Stephen Allinson has specialised in credit, debt, restructuring and insolvency work since 1987, and has extensive experience in dealing with the full range of these procedures. Prior to setting up his own consultancy, he was a Business Recovery and Insolvency partner at a major law firm heading up a team of over 50 legal professionals undertaking national debt and insolvency contracts in both the private and public sectors.

Stephen was appointed Chairman of the Board of The Insolvency Service in January 2017 and is also the Chairman of the Joint Insolvency Examination Board (JIEB); one of the Chairmen of the Methodist Church Disciplinary Process; a Tutor at the University of Law and formerly the Deputy Independent Examiner for the Institute and Faculty of Actuaries. He is the author of 'Enforcement of a Judgment', widely regarded as the leading practitioner work on this subject, and also a contributor to leading legal educational publications and practical insolvency texts in both the corporate and personal insolvency arenas.

The Corporate Insolvency and Governance Act 2020
– A Practical Guide

The Corporate Insolvency and Governance Act 2020
– A Practical Guide

Stephen Allinson. LL.B(Hons). FABRP. MCICM.
Solicitor and Licensed Insolvency Practitioner.
Chairman of the Board of the Insolvency Service.

Law Brief Publishing

Published 2020 by Law Brief Publishing, an imprint of Law Brief Publishing Ltd
30 The Parks
Minehead
Somerset
TA24 8BT

www.lawbriefpublishing.com

Paperback: 978-1-913715-12-0

This guide is dedicated to all those who have worked so hard to keep us safe in these challenging times and with my sincerest sympathy to all who have lost loved ones through this pandemic.

ACKNOWLEDGEMENTS

In writing this guide, I want to express my very sincere thanks to a number of people. Firstly, the Policy team at the Insolvency Service who were instrumental in bringing this Act to fruition in such a timely fashion, so the profession owes significant thanks to them. Secondly, particular thanks to Paul Bannister and Angela Crossley for their analysis, and to both Elizabeth Johnson and Jamie Howarth. Elizabeth and Jamie are both students of mine at the University of Law and have diligently proofread the text and corrected my drafting errors. Bethany Richards from the University Library team has also helped with some very valuable research. Finally, my huge gratitude to my wife, Glenys, for her continued and very patient support throughout the whole timescale of this project and for her excellent proof reading and questioning from a non-lawyer's perspective.

To all these persons I am really grateful, although any published errors are my own.

Stephen Allinson
July 2020
stcvc@allinsonlaw.com

CONTENTS

CHAPTER ONE
INTRODUCTION

"An Act to make provision about companies and other entities in financial difficulty; and to make temporary changes to the law relating to the governance and regulation of companies and other entities."

The Corporate Insolvency and Governance Act 2020 (referred to throughout this book as "the Act") has been described as potentially the most significant change to insolvency and restructuring law since the seminal Insolvency Act 1986. The 1986 Act created practices and procedures that are now very familiar to us, such as administration, corporate and personal voluntary arrangements and statutory demands. This Act creates two new corporate insolvency rescue procedures, as well as bringing into force other temporary and permanent insolvency reforms.

The immediate background to the Act is clearly the COVID-19 pandemic and has been born out of that hugely challenging situation, although some of the reforms are also based on the 2018 Government response to the consultation on Insolvency and Corporate Governance. At the daily coronavirus press conference on 28th March, the Secretary of State for BEIS, the Right Honourable Alok Sharma MP, announced a series of reforms to the insolvency process to counter the economic crisis the United Kingdom was facing. These proposals were then further developed by a press release, dated 23rd April, concerning winding up petitions and statutory demands.

In early June, the Insolvency Service published an overview of the Bill (as it then was) via a fact sheet and it can be found at:

https://www.gov.uk/government/publications/corporate-insolvency-and-governance-bill-2020-factsheets/overview-of-the-bill

After a period of very intense work, notably by the policy and legal teams in the Insolvency Service and related Government departments, the Bill received its first reading in the House of Commons on 20th May. It then progressed through Parliament in June.

It came into force on 26th June 2020 and this was the culmination of a very intense month for Parliament. The overarching objective of the Act is to create structures that will provide businesses with the flexibility and breathing space they need to continue trading and avoid insolvency during this period of economic uncertainty and beyond. It runs to almost 250 pages, and consists of 50 substantive sections and 14 Schedules. Many amendments to existing legislation are included, alongside completely novel provisions. This does make the navigation of the Act sometimes challenging, especially as there are also a series of carve outs and exceptions and exclusions to take account of, particularly in the financial services sector.

This book sets out the main areas of the insolvency and restructuring legislation in the Act, together with related provisions, and provides guidance on the practical and procedural application of the legislation. Inevitably, being published so soon after the Act has received Royal Assent, this book details the law prior to any testing from the courts. As is the nature of our legal system, court challenges will follow as the Judges interpret the law. In addition we can expect further guidance in the form of more detailed Rules, Practice Directions and Practice Statements. Indeed, we have already seen both a Temporary and Permanent Practice Direction issued as well as a Practice Statement to which reference will be made in the appropriate chapters.

The Act also needs to be considered against the backdrop of huge economic and personal uncertainty. At the time of writing in the summer of 2020, the UK is bracing itself for an economic downturn as the country seeks to move forward after the pandemic. Whether these new procedures aid in the recovery will become clear with time, but that is the rationale of the Act as announced by the Government.

It is interesting to note that the insolvency statistics, which are now produced monthly by the Insolvency Service, are showing a considerable drop in the number of formal appointments compared with similar periods in 2019. The June 2020 figures show that there were 732 company insolvencies in England and Wales. These comprised 557 creditors' voluntary liquidations; 61 compulsory liquidations; 100 administrations and 14 company voluntary arrangements. This total figure was 22% lower than the overall total in May which was 944 and 50% lower than the figure in June 2019. Most commentators believe this is the "lull before the storm" economically, and many insolvency and restructuring practices are preparing themselves for very busy periods of work. Economic and business experts predict a recession worse than the "credit crisis" of 2008/9.

Against this backdrop, what are the key headline provisions in the Act?

There are five main insolvency related measures included in the Act, together with some miscellaneous company reporting and filing changes. As stated earlier, the company rescue proposals had already been announced by the Government and were in development before Covid-19, through the 2018 Consultation on Insolvency and Corporate Governance. This was part of the (then) Government's focus on delivering a strong business environment in the UK. It sought views on ways to improve the insolvency rescue framework and also to reduce the risk of company failures occurring through poor governance or stewardship Some of the measures in the new Act arise directly out of the Government response to that 2018 consultation, although other ones, notably around the areas of greater potential consequences, both financial and otherwise, for directors, have not been implemented through this Act. Thus, what we now have are both permanent and temporary reforms to corporate insolvency and related processes.

In summary the provisions are:

1. Company Moratorium

The Act gives struggling businesses a formal breathing space to pursue a rescue plan. It creates a moratorium during which no legal action can be taken against a company without leave of the court. The decision to introduce the moratorium now is in order to ensure that companies that are struggling as a direct result of the pandemic are given the opportunity to survive. However, this is a permanent measure from the Act, albeit supplemented with some special temporary provisions.

2. Restructuring Plan

The provisions here are to enable viable companies struggling with debt obligations to restructure under a new procedure. It allows courts to sanction a plan that binds creditors to a restructuring plan if it is fair, equitable and in the interests of creditors. Creditors vote on the plan, but the court can impose it on dissenting creditors. It is similar to, but distinctive from, the existing Scheme of Arrangement which is laid out in the Companies Act 2006.

3. "Ipso Facto" (Termination) Clauses

When a company enters an insolvency or restructuring procedure, key suppliers will often either stop or threaten to stop supplying the company. The supply contract may well give them the right to do this, but doing that could materially jeopardise any attempt to rescue the business. The Act will ensure that suppliers will not be able to hinder a rescue in this way. There are safeguards to ensure that continued supplies are paid for, but there are protective mechanisms for suppliers if the requirement to supply causes hardship to their business. There are also some temporary provisions in the Act for "small company" suppliers during the pandemic.

4. Wrongful Trading Provisions

The Act potentially removes for a limited time personal liability arising from wrongful trading for directors who continue to trade a company through the crisis. It has been hailed by some commentators as a suspension of wrongful trading, but the provisions are not as simplistic as that. The clear intention is to remove the pressure on directors who may be tempted to place otherwise viable businesses into insolvency to avoid personal liability. All other potential director actions remain in place.

5. Statutory Demands and Winding up Petitions

The Act seeks to help struggling businesses by temporarily removing the threat of winding up proceedings where a debt is unpaid due to Covid-19. These are temporary provisions to void statutory demands issued against companies during the pandemic. This gives businesses the opportunity to reach agreements with creditors rather than face insolvency. In addition, extra checks on the issuance of winding up petitions and obtainment of winding up orders are introduced.

6. Company Law Reporting and Filing

Certain company law procedures have been temporarily relaxed including those around the holding of Annual General Meetings and corresponding filing requirements. Reference is made to these provisions in Chapter 9.

In terms of the territorial coverage, the Act contains provisions which apply in England, Wales, Scotland and Northern Ireland. This book will concentrate on the jurisdiction of England and Wales.

Inevitably, litigation surrounding these provisions will follow, and, where appropriate, this book makes reference to recent cases which may be indicative of how this area of law could progress. This is a very fast moving subject, however, so it is important to remain fully up to date with the inevitable case law and potential legislative changes. This is because the Act contains many and extensive powers for the Secretary of State to modify legislation as deemed necessary by way of further Regulations and other provisions. Such clauses are often interestingly called "Henry VIII" provisions, as legal historians will know, and reference to these is made throughout all relevant chapters.

The Insolvency Service recognised the significance of this area and published a factsheet when the Bill was first published. It can be found at:

https://www.gov.uk/government/publications/corporate-insolvency-and-governance-bill-2020-factsheets/delegated-powers

It is important to note that this document (as the other factsheets that were produced) pre-dated the full passage of the Bill through Parliament and so does not reflect the Parliamentary changes that took place before the Act received Royal Assent.

Finally, to complete the book, Chapter 10 looks at further changes and developments that are on the horizon in the insolvency and restructuring world.

The law, as I understand it, is accurate as at 31st July 2020.

CHAPTER TWO
MORATORIUMS UNDER THE CORPORATE INSOLVENCY AND GOVERNANCE ACT 2020

1. Introduction

The Act introduces a new restructuring tool into the Insolvency Act 1986 ("IA 1986") in the form of a free-standing and independent moratorium which it is intended to be commenced by directors through a relatively straightforward process. It is possibly the most significant of the five main insolvency measures introduced by the Act and so will be considered in the most detail in this book. The purpose of the moratorium is to provide a company in financial distress with breathing space to explore its restructuring options without the pressure (in the main) of creditor action. However, it should be noted that, whilst the moratorium is available for use by most types of companies, there are detailed eligibility requirements. To complicate matters further, some of the eligibility requirements have been relaxed temporarily to account for the effects of COVID-19. The temporary provisions surrounding the moratorium procedure will be considered in Chapter 3.

Fundamentally for this rescue procedure, the debtor company remains in possession on a day to day basis with the directors retaining control in most situations. However, it is still a formal insolvency procedure as an insolvency practitioner (called an "insolvency monitor") oversees the process. Some commentators have likened this to the company voluntary arrangement ("CVA") procedure where an insolvency practitioner is the Supervisor of the arrangement. Indeed, there is no doubt that there are similarities with the current small companies CVA moratorium provisions in Sch. A1 to the IA 1986, although these are very rarely used in practice.

The comparison is not strictly accurate, as there are also fundamental differences in the two procedures as will be explored later in this chapter. Furthermore, the Act makes it clear that the historical CVA moratorium provisions are to be repealed (Sch.3, para 2). Given the non-operation of these provisions in practice, nothing will turn on the loss of this procedure.

The new process is intended to exist independently of other insolvency processes, but time will tell if it will be utilised as a pre-cursor for some of the current well-established rescue procedures. Insolvency practitioners will inevitably develop their own commercial approach to this process.

2. Where to find the law

It is worth noting here that the structure of the whole Act throughout consists both of new provisions and also those that are inserted into other Acts, notably the IA 1986. This can make the process of cross referencing somewhat demanding and careful reading is often required.

The Act has created a new Part A1 to the IA 1986 which is the most detailed part of the Act (spanning nearly 70 pages). Part A1 is situated before Part 1 (but within the First Group of Parts). The new Part is made up of 8 Chapters, which set out the scope and details of the moratorium process.

The key provisions of the Act concerning moratoriums are:

- s.1, which includes the text of the new Part A1 for insertion into the IA 1986, comprising ss.A1-A55 and split into 8 Chapters;

- Sch.1, which sets out the text of the new Schedule ZA1 to the IA 1986;

- Sch.2, which sets out the text of Schedule ZA2 to the IA 1986;

- Sch.3, which sets out various consequential amendments to primary legislation; and

- Sch.4, which sets out the temporary provisions which apply as a response to COVID-19.

For ease of understanding, when referring to Sch.ZA1 and Sch.ZA2, this chapter and any following will not include the references to these being created through Sch.1 and Sch.2, but this should be taken as read. Similarly, references to the new Part A1 will stand on their own and it is not set out going forward that these are all created by s.1 of the Act.

However, all relevant parts of the Act concerning this new process should be considered when analysing the procedure itself. The Act applies to Great Britain and Northern Ireland as already mentioned, and the Northern Ireland sections and Schedules are set out separately in the Act. As mentioned in the opening Chapter, this guide covers the law as it applies in England and Wales, although there are many similarities with the new Northern Ireland legislation. The Scottish provisions reflect the substantive insolvency and related law in that country, but, again, there is considerable overlap with the

England and Wales legislation. The relevant provisions came into effect immediately upon the Act coming into force on 26th June 2020.

As with other provisions in the Act, the Insolvency Service has published a fact sheet (which actually pre-dates the Act, so care should be taken when referring to it) and it can be found at:

https://www.gov.uk/government/publications/corporate-insolvency-and-governance-bill-2020-factsheets/moratorium

As stated in the introduction to this chapter it is important to understand that the Act effectively introduces two new regimes: the permanent and new insolvency rescue procedure, and a temporary one responding to the COVID-19 crisis. The temporary provisions (as described in Chapter 3) create a modified version of the moratorium intended to have effect for a short period of time (s.3 confirms that these provisions are to be found in Sch.4 of the Act).

There are also many references in the Act to the Insolvency (England and Wales) Rules 2016 (SI 2016/1024) and related secondary legislation. Clearly these 2016 must be amended as they are the engine which will drive the operation of the moratorium. The Insolvency Service has produced guidance for monitors which can be found on the Insolvency Service website at:

https://www.gov.uk/government/publications/insolvency-act-1986-part-a1-moratorium-guidance-for-monitors

In addition, there is Companies House guidance regarding notification requirements. Details of the forms to be used can be found at:

https://www.gov.uk/government/collections/companies-house-moratorium-forms

However, and this is significant, the Act reserves extensive order-making powers to the Secretary of State to issue regulations on a wide range of matters arising out of the moratorium. To that end, we can expect several developments around this new process in the coming months. Already, a statutory instrument has been introduced to make the moratorium available for limited liability partnerships ("LLPs") and charitable incorporated organisations, with co-operative and community benefit societies expected to follow suit.

3. The moratorium: to whom will it apply?

A moratorium is available to any "**eligible company**". This definition is found in Sch.ZA1 as any company that is not excluded by:

- Having been subject to a moratorium or other insolvency procedure in the preceding 12 months: Sch.ZA1 para 2; and

- Carrying on business in an excluded category: Sch.ZA1 paras 3-22.

- The excluded categories largely comprise businesses within the financial services sector, i.e. banks, insurers and other monetary and capital markets institutions. It must not fall within this list.

- It will apply to LLPs, although surprisingly not Scottish LLPs.

- Further, it will include overseas companies, which are companies incorporated outside the UK and not excluded by Sch.ZA1, para 18

- Finally, it will include foreign and UK entities that are dealt with as "unregistered companies".

There are special rules for certain kinds of other companies, notably "regulated companies" as defined in the Act (see ss.A49, 50). There is also the power for the Secretary of State to make provisions in connection with pension schemes (s.A51).

It will be interesting to see whether the overseas provisions will change after 31ˢᵗ December 2020 when the UK formally leaves the European Union.

These exclusions are highly significant. Careful reference should be made to the financial services sector exclusions. The United Kingdom has a number of special and independent insolvency regimes in this arena which will remain unaffected. The Insolvency Service fact sheet on this area is a good reference point, although again it was issued before the Act received Royal Assent. It can be found at:

https://www.gov.uk/government/publications/corporate-insolvency-and-governance-bill-2020-factsheets/financial-services-exclusions

The previous insolvency procedure exclusion is also fundamental. The company must not have previously had a moratorium, entered into administration or a CVA, or had a winding up order or undischarged winding up petition made against it in the previous 12 months. There is a similar exclusion for administrative receivership (perhaps not relevant in practice) and the appointment of a provisional liquidator (which could be highly significant). This important provision is set out in Sch. ZA1, para 2.

4. The relevant criteria

The root test that is set out is that the moratorium is only available where a company is unable, or likely to become unable, to pay its debts and there is a likelihood of rescuing the company as a going concern. This is, of course, a well-established test in insolvency law. Therefore, the emphasis is very much on the company surviving and emerging as solvent from these difficulties rather than ending up in liquidation.

The directors are required to make a statement to the court that, in their view, the company is, or is likely to become, unable to pay its debts. This builds on the directors remaining in position and continuing to run the company.

However, it is for the monitor to confirm that it is likely that a moratorium would result in a rescue of the company as a going concern. Again, similarities can be seen between the wording here and in other insolvency rescue procedures. The interrelationship between the directors and the monitor will be fundamental and will no doubt be subject to much debate and analysis both procedural and judicial.

5. The monitor

The process will be overseen by one or more monitors (who will be a licensed insolvency practitioner and, as always in a formal insolvency appointment, an Officer of the Court). This is a new term in insolvency legislation and one with which practitioners are going to have to become familiar. One of the monitor's first tasks following the commencement of the moratorium is to notify all creditors and

Companies House of the moratorium, so the commencement of this process is publicly available. Company Information Agents and creditors will be reviewing their processes in light of this new procedure.

The monitor has an ongoing duty, and must continually assess whether it remains likely that the moratorium will result in the rescue of the company as a going concern (s.A35). If events develop in other ways separate duties come into play and the monitor "*must bring the moratorium to an end*" if they think that the company is no longer likely to be rescued as a going concern, or if various other ongoing conditions are met (s.A38).

No guidance is given as to how soon this duty is triggered and this will undoubtedly be interpreted differently by individual monitors on a commercial basis. As will be seen below, there are protections for creditors if they are unhappy at decisions that are taken (or not taken) by the monitor.

This is an interesting concept as the directors will remain in charge of the company generally and run the business on a day-to-day basis. It is important to compare this with the administration process. It remains to be seen what checks and balances the monitor will want following their appointment and how this may develop in practice. The thinking is that there will be "light touch supervision" by the monitor. Clearly there will have to be a great deal of trust by the monitor in the directors. Given the company is clearly in financial trouble and the actions of the directors may have contributed to this, some obvious tensions can be perceived.

The Act does not preclude the monitor from taking a later appointment as an administrator or liquidator. It is likely in practice that monitors will, in some instances, take such appointments. This is a fundamental change from the original proposal arising out of the 2018 consultation which proposed that the monitor could not take a subsequent administration or liquidation appointment for the company within 12 months of the end of the moratorium. This is perhaps a proposal that arises out of the current COVID-19 crisis. It is likely that monitors will wish to take such appointments, although, as always, that will be a commercial decision.

Clearly, many insolvency practitioners will be concerned about the costs of this procedure. Because of the nature of this process, the monitor's fees to be charged to the company are a private contract between those two parties. However, that is not to say that they will not be subject to future scrutiny. As will be seen later, if another formal insolvency process follows, an administrator or liquidator may have the power to challenge the monitor's fees if he or she is of the opinion that they are excessive. Reference should be made to the specific amendment to s.246ZD of the IA 1986 by Sch.3, para 16 of the Act which allows this cause of action to be pursued.

Of course, any monitor will also be concerned about his or her costs if the company does go into another formal insolvency process. Further information surrounding priority of debts is set out in section 11 below.

6. Practice and procedure

Entry into the moratorium will be triggered by filing the necessary papers at Court (a process resembling the current procedure for an out of court appointment of an administrator) unless the company is an overseas company or has a pending winding up petition, in which case there will need to be a Court hearing. The process is triggered when the actual order is made (s.A3).

Eligible companies that are subject to winding up petitions and eligible overseas companies are required to make an application to court in order to obtain a moratorium (ss.A4-A5).

Whether the appointment is made out of court or by a court application, the supporting documentation in s.A6 must be produced. Very importantly this includes a statement from the proposed monitor (s.A6 (1) (e)) which confirms that it is likely that the moratorium would result in the rescue of the company as a going concern. As we have seen this is the fundamental objective of a moratorium.

It is interesting that the Act does not deal with the position of a company that is subject to an outstanding creditor's administration application. Part A1 does not explicitly prevent a company subject to such an application from obtaining a moratorium out of court potentially in order to prevent a creditor bringing a hostile administration application. How this plays out in practice will be very interesting to see.

7. Length of the moratorium (ss.A9-A17)

The initial term of the moratorium is 20 business days, beginning the day after the moratorium comes into force. However, it is possible for this period to be extended in certain circumstances once by the directors, or otherwise with the approval of creditors or by the court.

There are various ways in which the moratorium can be extended, including:

i. by the directors unilaterally for one further period of 20 business days;

ii. by the directors with creditor consent for such a period as the creditors agree; and

iii. by the Court in its discretion.

In each case, there are requirements for confirmations to be made by the directors and/or the monitor regarding the payment of debts and the likelihood of the company's rescue. All moratorium debts must be paid, together with any other debts which are excluded from the moratorium.

The moratorium will also be extended if it is due to expire in the period between launch and approval or rejection of a CVA.

These provisions are set out in detail in ss.A10-A15.

In certain circumstances a moratorium may be terminated before it expires, most notably if the company enters into another relevant insolvency procedure (s.A16). For more information on termination see section 14 later in this chapter.

Immediately on the coming into force of the moratorium it is required to be publicised widely and all known creditors must be notified. Companies House notifications will be one of the first ports of call for anyone checking if a moratorium is in force.

8. Consequences and effects of the moratorium

There are clear obligations on directors to notify the monitor when a moratorium for the company is extended or comes to an end (s.A17). In practice, it is hard to believe that the monitor will not know, of course! The monitor also has notification duties, crucially to all creditors (and Companies House). This is a vital part of the procedure because a moratorium provides the financially troubled company with protection against creditor action. Insolvency professionals are very used to this concept as it is one that is afforded to companies in administration. However, it is not a complete carte blanche for the company once in a moratorium, as there are certain restrictions on what the directors of the company can do without the consent of the monitor or the Court, as will be seen below. Further, during this period the company must ensure that it pays certain types of pre- and post-moratorium debts, whilst receiving a "holiday" from the payment of other debts. These provisions are quite complex and promoted quite a lot of debate when the Bill was originally produced. Indeed, changes were made in this area as the Bill proceeded through Parliament.

These are potentially very important consequences for both the debtor company and the creditors. The effects can be found in ss.A18-A33 and the most important ones are summarised as follows:

i.   The suspension of various legal processes and execution against the company, similar to the moratorium accompanying administration (ss.A20-A23). Thus, there can be no winding up petitions, creditor enforcement action and legal processes, including forfeiture and other enforcement action by landlords, unless leave of the Court is obtained. This is clearly a wide protection as befits the theory of this process. Furthermore, uncrystallised floating charges cannot be crystallised during the moratorium (or as a result of a moratorium) and security cannot be enforced unless it falls within certain limited exceptions. This is quite significant as secured creditors' rights usually remain fully enforceable in other insolvency processes and demonstrates the power of the moratorium from the point of view of the debtor company.

ii. There are restrictions on certain transactions by the company, including obtaining credit of £500 or more, paying some pre-moratorium debts and disposing of property (ss.A25-A30). Each restriction contains exemptions and alternative options, so they need to be read carefully. The one that will be utilised the most will likely be the monitor giving their consent to the relevant actions. Again, therefore, there is an extra decision making onus on the monitor, but where the monitor's consent is required as a condition to the action such consent will only be given if the monitor thinks it will support the overarching requirement of rescuing the company as a going concern.

iii. Security may also be granted if the monitor consents. Consent will only be provided if the monitor thinks that the grant of security will support the rescue of the company.

iv. The Act gives the ability, with the permission of the court, to dispose of property free from charges, security interests or rights under hire purchase agreements that would otherwise apply (ss.A31 andA32). There is a clear statement that the court should only give this permission if it thinks that doing so will support the rescue of the company as a going concern. To create a situation where creditors will possibly lose their security interest has the potential to raise alarm bells. The Act creates compensatory provisions for secured creditors but will these be viewed as satisfactory by these creditors given what they are potentially losing?

v. There are prohibitions on entering into certain types of contracts such as market contracts and financial collateral arrangements.

Linked to these provisions are references to debt "payment holidays" which affect the priority of debts during the moratorium and in any subsequent insolvency proceedings (s.A18) (which will be considered later in section 10 of this Chapter).

Reference has already been made to the necessary publicity with which the company must comply (s.A19). As with other insolvency procedures, notice is to be given to all who need to know that the moratorium is in force and also the name of the appointed monitor. This notice must be displayed on the company's website, at all its places of business and on all business documents (such as invoices and order forms).

9. The (non) operation of s.127 IA 1986 (void nature of dispositions of property)

S.127 IA 1986 (avoidance of property dispositions after com-mencement of winding up) is dis-applied for the period a moratorium is in force (Sch.3 para 12).

In its place, the moratorium creates limited restrictions on disposi-tions of property (s.A29) which allow a company to dispose of property in the ordinary course of business, where the monitor con-sents (or the disposal is pursuant to a court order). As insolvency professionals are aware, s.127 allows property transferred in breach of the restriction to be recovered. There is, perhaps surprisingly, no linked provision in this regime. Given the importance of s.127 for insolvency practitioners this may potentially be a significant limit-ation.

10. **Moratorium debts**

This is a very important concept to understand and to a certain extent there is a need for new understanding. The first term to understand is the "payment holiday". This was mentioned in section 8 above, but, in simple terms, the Act introduces a provision whereby a company in a moratorium does not have to pay during this process for the majority of debts which fall due before the moratorium commenced or during the moratorium.

As one would expect, there are exceptions to this payment holiday set out in the Act.

To understand the process, it is important to first appreciate that the Act classifies debts initially as being pre-moratorium debts or moratorium debts:

i. Pre-moratorium debts are debts or liabilities to which the company is subject: (i) before the moratorium; or (ii) during the moratorium, by reason of an obligation incurred before the moratorium came into effect (s.A53 (1)).

ii. Moratorium debts are debts or liabilities to which the company becomes subject during or after the moratorium, by reason of an obligation incurred during the moratorium (s.A53 (2)). Clearly this could include company borrowing which will be considered later in this chapter at section 12.

The Act then further splits this classification into:

• Pre-moratorium debts subject to a payment holiday; and

• Pre-moratorium debts not subject to a payment holiday.

Different consequences apply depending on in which category the debt comes under.

The categories of pre-moratorium debts not subject to a payment holiday are defined in s.A18 (3) as amounts due in respect of:

(a) the monitor's remuneration or expenses;

(b) goods or services supplied during the moratorium;

(c) rent in respect of a period during the moratorium;

(d) wages or salary arising under a contract of employment;

(e) redundancy payments (including holiday and sick pay and occupational pension scheme payments); or

(f) debts or other liabilities arising under a contract or other instrument involving financial services, as defined in Sch.ZA2.

Logically then, all other pre-moratorium debts are pre-moratorium debts subject to a payment holiday, again via s.A18 (3).

The range of liabilities excluded from the payment holiday provisions is significant and the categories are broad. There has been much discussion around category (vi) above, being what is known as the "financial services" exception and it is so widely drafted that it could be interpreted as including not only traditional bank lending but also private funding which could include directors' loans. The operation of directors' loans is always a keen area for insolvency practitioners to consider.

11. **Priority of debts**

Having established the different categories, the Act then provides for the different treatment of them in several respects.

A moratorium not only relieves the company of the obligation to pay pre-moratorium debts subject to a payment holiday, it actually restricts a company's ability so to do (s.A28). Payments which exceed £5,000 or 1% of the total debt (whichever is the greater) may only be made with a monitor's consent, a court order or where payment is required by ss. A31 (3) or A32 (3) (payments to creditors following disposal of property subject to a security interest or a hire purchase agreement).

This is to be contrasted with how a company must treat moratorium debts and pre-moratorium debts not subject to a payment holiday which fall due during the moratorium. Fundamentally, payment of such debts is a precondition of an extension to the moratorium beyond the initial 20 business day period (see section 7 above).

This does not apply, though, to automatic extensions pending a decision on CVA proposals or schemes of arrangement.

This is a result of the combined effect of ss.A10 (1) (b), A11 (1) (b) and

A13 (2) (a). If any of these debts are not paid then it is a ground to terminate a moratorium (s.A38 (1) (d)).

There are then the provisions that will apply if a company goes into liquidation or administration as a consequence of a resolution, application or petition presented before the moratorium, or within 12 weeks following the end of a moratorium. In these circumstances, both moratorium debts and pre-moratorium debts not subject to a payment holiday, will be paid in preference to other claims, with Sch.3 para 13 stating that rules may make provision to the order in which these debts rank among themselves define the order of the priority for those debts within themselves. This will be important for the insolvency practitioner as his or her unpaid costs are included in these categories. Sch.4, containing the temporary monitor provisions actually does set out that priority (see Sch.4 para 42) and this is further considered in Chapter 3.

These are quite complex provisions. In summary, the costs incurred by the company during a moratorium will be given "super-priority" on administration or liquidation, including priority over any costs, claims or expenses in the administration or liquidation. There are also certain restrictions in relation to the compromise of unpaid moratorium debts within other insolvency procedures, namely a CVA or a restructuring plan.

What is significant, therefore, is that the moratorium alters the priority of debts in a subsequent liquidation or administration which will undoubtedly have a significant impact on the level of recovery likely to be made by creditors if the company ultimately fails. How will creditors respond to this once the procedure has settled down over the coming months? What about lending institutions? Will they seek to make formal demand on any loans or overdrafts which become due during the moratorium period in order to protect their lending? The position of lenders is considered below and then in more detail in Chapter 4.

12. Borrowing during the moratorium

As has been described earlier, the debtor company is able, under certain circumstances, to enter into new borrowing arrangements during the moratorium. However, s.A25 makes it clear that credit of

£500 or more can only be obtained if the person or institution has been informed that a moratorium is in force. This is a low threshold and covers all except minimal borrowing.

Further, s.A26 (1-2) also allows security to be granted, but only if the monitor consents and to give that consent they must believe that the grant of security will support the rescue of the company as a going concern. These new liabilities, secured or unsecured will be treated as "moratorium debts" and will therefore take complete priority over other liabilities (other than fixed charge security) if the company goes into liquidation or administration within 12 weeks after the end of the moratorium. Furthermore, CVAs Schemes of Arrangement or other new restructuring plans commenced in the same time period cannot compromise these liabilities.

So, how will the relevant parties approach these provisions? Will the monitor be confident to consider further borrowing? What role will they play in the company's decision to require it? The Act states that a monitor's agreement is technically not needed for any fresh unsecured lending incurred during the moratorium. Surely, however, in terms of carrying out their professional role, the monitor will wish to be completely involved with the process. Ultimately, if he or she is not satisfied that this extra borrowing could be repaid in accordance with the terms created, then there must be a discussion around whether there are grounds for the termination of the moratorium, with all the significant issues that would raise. Once again, there are some very important commercial decisions to be taken into account by the monitor.

What of the lender itself? As stated above, the position will be considered in Chapter 4, but there are also important commercial decisions to be taken by those approached to further fund the potential rescue.

13. Challenges to the monitor's actions

A creditor, director, or member of the company, or any other person affected by the moratorium, may apply to the court if their interests have been unfairly harmed by an act, omission or decision of the monitor (s.A42 (1)-(2)) and an application may be made during the moratorium or after it has ended (s.A42(3)). The court can confirm, reverse or modify any act of the monitor, or give directions, but cannot order the monitor to pay compensation (s.A42 (4)). This should be of particular comfort to the insolvency practitioner.

It seems that the areas of challenge are not limited and presumably would include the failure by the monitor to terminate the moratorium by not following the provisions of s.A38 (see section 14 below). Again, one can see potential litigation challenges regarding this part of the Act.

Creditors or members can also challenge the moratorium on the grounds that the company's affairs, business and property are being or have been managed in a way that has unfairly harmed the interests of its creditors or members or that any act or proposed omission causes or would cause such harm (s.A44). Perhaps this can be viewed as closely replicating the well-established challenges that are available under the CVA procedure.

As mentioned earlier in this chapter, s.A43, states that rules may be laid to confer on an administrator or liquidator the right to apply to the court on the ground that the remuneration charged by the monitor in relation to a prior moratorium for the company was excessive.

Finally, s.A45 gives specific rights of challenge to be brought by the Board of the Pension Protection Fund. This provision is consistent with various concerns expressed whilst the Bill was debated about ensuring proper protection for pension funds. Changes were brought in as the Bill proceeded through the House of Lords, in particular.

14. Termination of the moratorium

Pursuant to the Act, the moratorium will be terminated in the following circumstances:

i. Effluxion of time.

ii. The company enters into a compromise or arrangement with its creditors (e.g. a scheme of arrangement or a restructuring plan) or otherwise enters into an insolvency procedure (e.g. a CVA administration or liquidation).

By s.A38, the monitor files notice with the Court in certain circumstances. These are where, in the monitor's opinion, the moratorium is no longer likely to result in the rescue of the company as a going concern; the rescue has been achieved, or where the monitor cannot carry out its functions or believes that the company cannot pay the debts. None of these circumstances are surprising given the way the scheme is intended to operate but (iii) above, once again, places the onus squarely on the monitor.

15. Conclusion

The new moratorium provisions are a brand new addition to the insolvency and restructuring world. Business groups have been very supportive of the approach. The new legislation under the Act has some significant changes to the original proposal of the 2018 consultation, due to the need to respond to the COVID-19 pandemic.

As the first applications and orders are made and potential challenges in the courts on various aspects of the scheme follow, further clarifications on some of the more contentious areas may well follow. The "debtor in possession" concept is not new and the appointment of a monitor means that the directors do not have free reign once a moratorium is in place. Will this satisfy the creditors? One clear check on the directors is the need in practice for creditor or court approval for an extended moratorium of longer than 40 business days. It is anticipated that this will ensure the directors will appropriately engage with the monitor and creditors throughout. The terms of the engagement for the monitor will also serve to make this requirement clear. This could be easier for the smaller owner-managed business than larger companies and they may consider that the new restructuring tool is more appropriate to their needs.

We must not underestimate the significance of the exclusion of several financial contracts from the moratorium's scope. The requirement under the scheme to pay banks and other financial liabilities that are due both before and during the initial moratorium period if it is to be extended could be a real factor in the success of this process. The position of a lender to the company is considered later in Chapter 4.

CHAPTER THREE
TEMPORARY PROVISIONS CONCERNING MORATORIUMS UNDER THE CORPORATE INSOLVENCY AND GOVERNANCE ACT 2020

1 Introduction

The permanent provisions of the moratorium have been considered in detail in Chapter 2. However, the Act also creates a modified version, and this is intended to have effect for a short period of time. The relevant law here can be found in Sch.4 of the Act for the Great Britain provisions. Separate provisions are set out for Northern Ireland, just as for the permanent regime. These can be found in Sch. 8 and should be read separately. This book will concentrate on the Great Britain provisions.

2 Why have these temporary provisions been introduced?

Prior to the introduction of these provisions detailed further proposals were discussed by senior leaders in the policy team of the Insolvency Service and discussed with various business groups. The thrust of these representations was effectively that the concept of "rescuability" for the company, which is one of the key components of the permanent regime, is a very difficult test to manage in the current situation. Thus, certain provisions temporarily relax, the permanent requirements in several respects. As will be discussed in the book, this is not the only temporary provision introduced by this Act.

3 Length of time for the temporary regime

The Act stipulates that the temporary regime will end on 30 September 2020, having commenced on the 26th June, the day the Act came into force.

However, this is subject to a general power to change the duration of, or switch off, the temporary provisions (Sch.4, paras 1-3). It is important, therefore, to track any potential changes to the duration over the immediate months.

The relevant Schedule is split into 4 Parts:

- Part 1 – setting out the "relevant period" and the powers to turn off temporary provisions;

- Part 2 – setting out modifications to primary legislation;

- Part 3 – setting out the temporary rules for England and Wales; and

- Part 4 – setting out the temporary rules for Scotland.

4 Comparison with the permanent regime

The clear purpose of this temporary regime is to make it easier for companies, which would in normal times be considered viable, but due to the pandemic are facing significant financial challenges, to access the moratorium regime. Several changes are thus created to the new permanent moratorium criteria. These are set out in Sch.4, Part 2, paras 6-10. They include:

i. A moratorium can be sought out of court, even where a winding up petition is outstanding.

ii. A moratorium may be granted, extended or permitted to continue even where, because of the worsening of the company's position due to COVID-19, the monitor cannot confirm that rescue as a going concern is likely. Thus, analysing that provision, the monitor must now only be of the view that a rescue would be possible were it not for any worsening of the financial position of the company for reasons relating to coronavirus. This provision is a significant deviation from the permanent regime where the test of rescuing the company as a going concern is fundamental and overarching.

iii. A company will be eligible if it has been the subject of a moratorium or another insolvency procedure, in practice an administration or company voluntary arrangement in the preceding 12 months (as long as it is not so subject at the filing date). Again, this removes one of the key criteria from the permanent moratorium requirements.

There is an additional exclusion from eligibility, set out in Sch.4, para 5 where certain regulated companies which may hold money for clients will not be eligible for a moratorium during this period. This is an extension to the original eligibility provisions set out in ss.A3, 4 or 5.

5   Temporary Amendment of the Insolvency (England and Wales) Rules 2016

As was mentioned in the introductory chapter, there are many provisions giving the Secretary of State the power to issue regulations and amend rules to ensure the new Act operates as required. This creates wide powers for sections in the Act to be amended without the need to return to Parliament for primary legislation.

For these temporary moratorium provisions, Sch.4, paras 12-51 of the Act (Part 3 of the Schedule) sets out, as would be expected, temporary modifications to the Insolvency Rules, which will cease to exist at the end of the temporary period, although there is also the power to bring in rules under s.411 IA 1986 to declare that any of these provisions cease to have effect before the end of the relevant period. These rules provide the way the temporary scheme will operate in practice. The amendments are detailed and will have to be considered carefully by practitioners wanting to invoke this regime while it is in force.

One very practical rule is worth mentioning. For monitors, it appears under the temporary regime that their own remuneration and expenses will rank below all other moratorium debts in a subsequent administration or liquidation (Sch.4, paragraphs 42 and 43). This is presumably to protect the integrity of the moratorium considering the significant intervention it brings in creditors rights.

It is interesting to note that, at the time of the Act commencing, the equivalent modifications of the Rules in relation to the permanent moratorium regime are not yet in force. However, we can expect these as the Act beds down. Similar temporary rules for Scotland are set out in Sch.4, paras 52-90, given the different insolvency processes that apply in relation to England and Wales.

6   Conclusion

It is hoped, for the good of the economy and business generally, that these provisions will not have to be extended as that would indicate the ongoing economic crisis was perhaps deeper than was at first envisaged. It is quite clear why the Government wanted the temporary regime, but some commentators have argued that this is running counter to the whole thrust of the moratorium purpose because it is not actually creating a vehicle for the rescue of the company. The clear purpose of the moratorium is to give time for an insolvency practitioner to explore, with the directors, the opportunity of the company' survival as a going concern. So, is the temporary regime going to be utilised by a company and its directors simply to "buy time" when the reality is that rescue is unlikely? Perhaps that is still a better option than immediate liquidation. Many in the insolvency and restructuring professions will be carefully reviewing the potential use of the temporary provisions.

CHAPTER FOUR
MORATORIUMS AND THE LENDER UNDER THE CORPORATE INSOLVENCY AND GOVERNANCE ACT 2020

1 Introduction

Chapters 2 and 3 have concentrated on the moratorium and its operation on a general legal and practical basis. Clearly a lender (secured or otherwise) is a very relevant player in this process, so it is important to consider how the new procedure may affect their position. In recent years, insolvency professionals have become very used to significant legal developments and case law around borrowing and security questions, particularly in administration, and the role of a secured creditor as a qualifying floating charge holder ("QFCH") or otherwise. A key question to ask might be of what both secured and unsecured lenders should be aware in this new rescue process?

It is also significant that, for secured lenders, some changes were made to the Bill as it passed through Parliament, and the Act as finally brought into force had different consequences for lenders than was originally drafted.

The fact that financial services contracts generally are considered so important in this Act is demonstrated by the fact that Sch. 2 to the Act introduced a new Sch.ZA2 to the IA Act 1986 which immediately follows Sch.ZA1, the provisions of which have been referred to regularly in Chapter 2. Sch.ZA2 is entitled "Moratoriums In Great Britain: Contracts Involving Financial Services".

2   Lenders and the entry into the moratorium

As we have seen, a moratorium can be entered into by simply filing documents at court. However, this is not always the case and sometimes a court order will be required, most commonly where there is an existing winding up petition in existence (see Chapter 2). Unlike the administration process, there is no requirement to notify or obtain the consent of a QFCH or other secured lender before the commencement of the moratorium process. Rather, a QFCH must be notified of the moratorium by the monitor, as well as other creditors once the moratorium is in force. Therefore, unlike in an administration, a QFCH will not at this stage be able to challenge the directors' choice of monitor.

We have also seen that there are opportunities to extend the moratorium beyond the initial 20 business days for a further 20 business days by the directors and for up to 12 months with creditor (or court) consent. The required creditor consent provisions are set out in ss.A11 and 12 and effectively it is those pre moratorium creditors for which the company has a payment holiday and which has not been paid or discharged. Any debt arising from a loan agreement and other financial documents has to be paid during the moratorium (see section 3 below), so it must follow that lenders who have lent in those circumstances do not take part in that extension voting process.

3   Lenders and payment during the moratorium

A fundamental aspect of the moratorium process is the protection for the company from paying pre-moratorium debts that have fallen due by the payment holiday provisions. This is a wide protection and includes debts that are also due during the moratorium. These provisions were considered in Chapter 2, section 10.

But there are exceptions to these payment holiday provisions and significantly one of those exceptions is that any debt and other liabilities arising under a contract or other instrument involving financial services (see s.A18 (3)) and Sch.ZA2). Logically, therefore, a company subject to a moratorium has to keep up with the required capital and interest payments under the terms of the borrowing. It must always be open to the company (and by extension, the monitor) to seek a temporary non-payment arrangement on a contractual basis, outside of the normal moratorium rules. In practice, though, why should the lender agree?

The sanction that exists for the company if it doesn't make these payments is that the monitor must consider whether the moratorium should continue. Therefore, it is very important to keep the lender on side in these circumstances.

There are also consequences to this categorisation if an insolvency process follows (see Sch.3 of the new Act which introduces several amendments to the IA 1986 and other legislation). The Act introduces a further "subcategory" within pre-moratorium debts, namely "priority pre-moratorium debts". This is effectively a somewhat narrower category of pre-moratorium debts without a payment holiday and these debts are able to gain priority or protection in the subsequent insolvency process that follows in the 12 week period after the end of the moratorium.

The key point for lenders is that amounts due under a contract or other instrument involving financial services are not included in priority pre-moratorium debts if they fell due before or during the moratorium because of the operation or exercise of an acceleration or early termination clause. For more detail on this see section 6 below.

4   Lenders and their ability to enforce payment

Although lenders' debts must still be paid during the moratorium because of the provisions above, if payment is not made, they will wish to be clear on their enforcement options. These are actually somewhat limited by the new Act.

The moratorium suspends a QFCH's ability to crystallise its charge or appoint an administrator (s.A22) and under the moratorium, charge holders are unable to enforce security without the consent of the court (s.A21 (1) (c). There are also some financial market exceptions which, as has been seen, are present in other areas of this Act as well.

5   Other options for the secured lender

A company cannot dispose of property subject to fixed charge security without court consent. However, directors may apply to the court to dispose of property as if it were not subject to the fixed charge (s.A31). There are provisions providing fixed charge holders with compensation for their loss of rights (effectively reimbursing the lender for what the court thinks the property would be worth in the open market). However, this effectively enables a restructuring package to ignore the security and could result in fixed charge holders being put at a significant disadvantage, with a loss of rights.

For floating charge assets, a company can either (a) deal with assets in accordance with the terms of the floating charge instrument; or (b) obtain consent of the court to deal with the assets in another way. As the floating charge cannot be crystallised, as mentioned in section 4 above, floating charge assets can usually be disposed of in the ordinary course of business (which presumably would be in accordance with the terms of the floating charge document). The potential consequences of this could be to reduce the assets remaining for a lender ahead who may be looking to those for future (post moratorium) enforcement considerations. Under the Act, once assets have been sold, the floating charge will simply remain over the proceeds of sale.

6   The interaction of the moratorium with the lender's rights

Although a QFCH cannot appoint an administrator during the moratorium, as set out above, the moratorium will automatically terminate upon the directors filing a notice of intention to appoint administrators (s.A16 (3) (c)). One has to question why the directors would consider taking that step. However, at that point, the QFCH would be able to exercise its powers as usual and regain control of the appointment process by appointing a replacement insolvency practitioner as administrator. Effectively, normal administration procedures are then resumed. Given that lenders often wish to control the process, the fact that these options are back in play is potentially significant.

Entering into a moratorium will in many cases constitute a default under the terms of the lending contract, although the contract will have to be carefully analysed. It will often mean that the whole debt will become due through the operation of the normal acceleration provisions. Lenders should update their contracts and deeds to ensure that a moratorium is an event of default triggering those automatic acceleration provisions.

Even in a situation where acceleration is not automatic, it may be open to lenders to force the issue to accelerate their debt by serving a formal notice so that it is payable on demand during the moratorium period. That act will almost inevitably trigger further actions as it would be unlikely that the company would pay. The onus would then be on the monitor who would effectively be put to an election. The choice is either to bring the moratorium to an end because they would consider that the company could not be rescued as a going concern, or to continue to support the process. Inevitably, if the decision is taken to continue with the process there will be detailed negotiations between the company and the lender. The aim must be to obtain a stay of any enforcement options by the lender. Again, the role and reputation of the monitor will be crucial.

If a stay cannot be agreed, it could be that the lender is in pole position and may trigger an administration appointment or other enforcement process if (or when) the moratorium is brought to an end in accordance with the Act.

In addition, there may be some other practical options open to lenders. Lenders should consider as part of their negotiation process whether, as a condition for providing additional lending they wish to retain further and more wide ranging security. The monitor's consent will, of course, be required. Further, as creditors, lenders can always challenge the conduct of the directors or the monitor at court, as set out in Chapter 2 when the role and responsibilities of the monitor were considered.

Finally, as will be discussed in Chapter 6, the Act also introduced some new and more stringently drafted "ipso facto" provisions preventing termination of contracts upon insolvency (see ss.14-19 of the Act and the related Sch.12 and Sch.13 for the changes in both Great Britain and Northern Ireland). The Act, as in other areas, provides exceptions to these provisions concerning financial services providers. This is a consistent theme. Will lenders use these exceptions to their advantage?

7   How will lenders' debts be ranked in a subsequent insolvency?

When the legislation was first drafted it gave priority status to all pre-moratorium debts without a payment holiday, but concerns were raised that the exercise of acceleration rights by financial creditors (as referred to above) could allow them to gain "super priority" for the full amount due to them and thus be in a better position in the event of a subsequent insolvency. As has been seen, it is perfectly possible to see how a lender could act so as to force a struggling company into further difficulty, thus leaving the monitor with no option but to terminate the moratorium.

An amendment was therefore suggested to remove the lender's ability to accelerate their debt during a moratorium. This was not accepted by the Government. Therefore, lenders are still able to accelerate their debt and bring serious pressure on the company and the monitor.

However, one amendment was agreed through the Parliamentary process to remove the priority of accelerated debt if the company enters into liquidation or administration within 12 weeks following the end of the moratorium.

As discussed in Chapter 3, the Act implements a number of amendments to existing insolvency legislation to alter the priority of distributions, where a company enters into administration or liquidation within 12 weeks of the moratorium ending. The amendments create a new order for moratorium debts and pre-moratorium debts that should have been paid during the moratorium. This would include lenders' debt. These are to be paid ahead of the normal distribution order in a liquidation or administration where preferential creditors are paid first. Interestingly, the amendments set out in Sch.3, paras 13, 14 and 31 and related provisions do not provide a ranking process within themselves for moratorium or pre moratorium debts, but confirm that Regulations can be brought into force to create that ranking.

So, what is the effect of these amendments in practice? We now have a clear distinction between non-accelerated bank and other lenders' debt falling due and payable during the moratorium, which retains this "super-priority" position. However, this is not the same for accelerated bank and lenders' debt which will no longer be paid on this "super-priority basis". Rather, this is to be paid as part of the normal floating charge distributions, which rank below the preferential creditors. Given that the relevant provisions of the Finance Act 2020 restoring the preferential status for HMRC from 1st December 2020 have just been confirmed, this amendment could be significant for lenders.

In addition, by Sch.3, para 4, Company Voluntary Arrangement proposals submitted within 12 weeks of the moratorium ending cannot provide for debts payable during the moratorium to be paid otherwise than in full. Similarly, any restructuring plan applied for within 12 weeks of the moratorium ending, cannot compromise moratorium expenses (or pre-moratorium debts without a payment holiday) without first obtaining the consent of each of these creditors (see Chapter 5). Again, these could be significant provisions for the lender to consider and build into any lending strategy.

We have already seen that there are some temporary moratorium provisions in this Act as a response to the COVID-19 crisis and, amongst other changes, these temporary provisions also provide clear statements on the order of priority for debts payable under the moratorium to be paid in a subsequent administration or liquidation. By these provisions, and with reference to Sch. 4, Part 3, para

42, lenders' debt would rank ahead of the monitor's remuneration and expenses, but behind suppliers who are covered by the aforesaid "ipso facto" provisions and employment-related costs.

8   Conclusion

Going forward, lenders will undoubtedly have to consider the consequences of a company taking advantage of the moratorium and build those consequences into their "take on" procedures as part of the overall risk analysis. A moratorium appointment may well be considered a "hostile" one by the lender as their consent is not necessary before the process commences.

Therefore, lawyers acting for lenders will be advising them to review their suite of products and, in particular, all standard terms of security and lending facilities to ascertain whether adequate protection exists given the two new rescue procedures. The inability of a lender to crystallise a floating charge or otherwise enforce security during a moratorium is a huge change from the normal protections that afforded in an administration process.

In turn, this may well mean that lenders become much more concerned at taking proper and clearly defined fixed charge security with all the advantages that come with that in terms of realisation options.

In practical terms, it is submitted that full dialogue between lender and corporate borrower is crucial (which could include the monitor). Their interests should be as one, in that it is normally the case that lenders have the best chance of protecting their investment in a company that trades moving forward, rather than one that faces administration or liquidation.

CHAPTER FIVE
RESTRUCTURING PLANS UNDER THE CORPORATE INSOLVENCY AND GOVERNANCE ACT 2020

1. Introduction

The Act introduces a completely new and flexible restructuring arrangement for companies in financial difficulty. This is known as the Restructuring Plan ("the Plan"). The legislation governing this Plan will sit alongside an existing restructuring tool, namely, the Scheme of Arrangement.

The new law can be found at s.7 and Sch.9 in the Act. Part 1 of Sch.9 contains the main provisions and Part 2 the consequential amendments flowing therefrom. It creates a new Part 26A to the Companies Act 2006. This new Part sits immediately after Part 26 and amends the Companies Act by inserting ss.901A-901L into that Act. Therefore, this is not an Insolvency Act 1986 procedure, but rather the substantive law is all included in the Companies Act 2006.

For ease of referencing going forward (as with other earlier referencing for the moratorium), references will be to the amended legislation in the Companies Act 2006.

Schemes of Arrangements are well known to corporate practitioners and have been a successful financial restructuring tool over recent years. They became very much mainstream after the financial problems that were seen in the last recession in 2007/8 and the following years.

This new Plan was originally proposed as part of the 2018 reforms which have been referred to earlier. However, the legislation has now been enacted in a different form from what was envisaged then and so it reflects some further development of thinking. On 14th July, Virgin Atlantic Airways announced that it had launched a restructuring plan using this process to implement a solvent recapitalisation and hoped that it would take effect in late summer 2020.

It is also important to understand that although the Plan is similar to the existing law on Schemes of Arrangement, it does not mirror it completely. Therefore, although there have been a number of important reported cases on the existing law, and detailed academic and practical analysis also exists, this law should be considered in its own right. By way of comparison, however, there was a Scheme of Arrangement case reported very recently, *Re ColourOz Investment 2 LLC and other companies (2020) EWHC 1864*. That case was a good example of the court responding to the COVID-19 situation and it gave a longer period of notice than normal for the convening hearing.

Some commentators have also drawn parallels for the new Plan with the established company voluntary arrangement ("CVA") procedure. This procedure is currently being used particularly in the retail sectors, with a number of high profile commercial tenants seeking rent reductions with their landlords through this method. It remains to be seen if commercial companies in the future consider the Plan as an alternative to the CVA. This could be the case because, as will be seen below, there is an opportunity to bind the dissatisfied creditors (such as the landlords) into the scheme.

Further, by way of introduction, it should also be noted that there are various references to the future development of rules and regulations under the control of the Secretary of State for this process.

Again, this is consistent with what we have seen in the drafting of the moratorium legislation so it is important to keep fully up to date with any future changes.

Similarly to the way the moratorium provisions developed through the parliamentary process, a number of changes developed as a result of lobbying and debate in both Houses. Amendments were introduced to make the aircraft industry subject of the Plan. Further, the Pensions Regulator and Pension Protection Fund (PPF) now has a part to play in the Plan. In addition, s.901I introduces a future power to make regulations enabling the PPF to exercise creditor rights held by the trustees or managers of pension schemes in relation to the Plan.

In the same vein, the Act gives the power for Secretary of State Regulations to provide that the Plan does not apply to companies providing financial services as defined in s.901B.

The Insolvency Service has produced a factsheet on this part of the Act (and others) and it can be found at:

https://www.gov.uk/government/publications/corporate-insolvency-and-governance-bill-2020-factsheets/restructuring-plan

This was actually produced when the Bill was first set before Parliament and so does not currently deal with all the subsequent changes. It does, however, state that regulations are expected to extend the current Plan provisions to include charitable incorporated organisations (CIOs); mutuals (including co-operatives and community benefit societies) and limited liability partnerships (LLPs). Currently the procedure is available to all companies which can be wound up under the provisions of Parts IV and V of the Insolvency Act 1986, and this will include unregistered companies.

As with current schemes of arrangement and the moratorium company criteria, overseas companies will be able to propose a Plan. They have to fit the test of being "liable to be wound up" under the Insolvency Act 1986. That long and well established test is one of "sufficient connection" to our jurisdiction, and the obvious connection is where assets still remain in this country. Again, as with the moratorium provisions, it will be interesting to see how this develops after 31st December 2020.

Finally, when considering this area, reference should not only be made to the Act, but also a Practice Statement for the Plan produced by the Chancellor of the High Court on the 26th June 2020, the day the Act came into force. This replaces the 2002 Practice Statement and covers the practice to be followed for both Part 26 and Part 26A court applications. It can be found at the following link:

https://www.judiciary.uk/wp-content/uploads/2020/06/Schemes-Practice-Statement-FINAL-25-6-20.pdf

The purpose of this Statement is, according to the opening paragraph, "to enable issues concerning the jurisdiction of the court to sanction the scheme, the composition of classes of creditors and/or members and the convening of meetings to be identified and if appropriate resolved early in the proceedings."

It then sets out the relevant practice to be followed and so is required reading for any lawyer practising in this arena.

2. What is the Plan in summary form?

The Plan involves a compromise or arrangement between the company and its creditors or members (or any class of them). It is the second measure created by the Act to support companies that are potentially viable but struggling with current ongoing debt and other obligations. Just like the moratorium, it is a rescue process. If the Plan works, a restructuring effectively takes place. It is a court process with the overarching requirement that it has to be fair and equitable for creditors. As is normal for insolvency procedures there is a vote for the Plan to be accepted, but the novel characteristic here is that it can be made binding by the court on a class of dissenting creditors. This is the process known as a "cross-class cram down" which is considered in section 5 below.

It is also a remedy that can be used by a variety of parties, as it may be proposed by the company, its creditors, shareholders, liquidators or administrators. Normally one would expect it to be initiated by the company itself, after consultation with solicitors and insolvency practitioners.

3. The criteria in more detail

The Plan will only apply to potentially insolvent companies. The test as set out is whether the company "has encountered, or is likely to encounter, financial difficulties that are affecting, or will or may affect, its ability to carry on business as a going concern" (s.901A (2)). By extension, therefore, it does not apply to solvent companies.

The Act then sets out a second condition, namely that a compromise or arrangement is proposed between the company and (a) its creditors, or any class of them; or (b) its members, or any class of them; and the purpose of the compromise or arrangement is to eliminate, reduce or prevent, or mitigate the effect of, any of those financial difficulties. (s.901A (3))

We should contrast this with a Scheme of Arrangement. These are used for various different types of corporate transactions to include solvent restructurings or corporate takeovers.

4 The process in practice

(Note: this analysis is taken from the combined reading of the Act and the recent Practice Statement referred to in the introduction).

The Plan process is very similar to a Scheme, broadly comprising

    i. an application to court and initial notice to stakeholders:

    ii. a convening hearing and notice to stakeholders together with an explanatory statement setting out details of the Plan;

    iii. stakeholder meetings to vote on the Plan, and

    iv. a sanction hearing. The court will scrutinise the fairness and reasonableness of the process, as well as ensuring that all procedural aspects have been satisfactorily undertaken.

(See ss.901C-901G).

An application will be made to a High Court Judge, (ideally the same one will preside over both hearings)) under s.901C to initiate the process.

Paragraph 6 of the Practice Statement states:

> **"It is the responsibility of the applicant, by evidence in support of the application or otherwise, to draw to the attention of the court at the hearing for an order that meetings of creditors and/or members be held ("the convening hearing"):**

a. any issues which may arise as to the constitution of meetings of members or creditors or which otherwise affect the conduct of those meetings;

b. any issues as to the existence of the court's jurisdiction to sanction the scheme;

c. (in relation to a Part 26A scheme) any issues relevant to the conditions to be satisfied pursuant to section 901A of the 2006 Act and, if an application under section 901C (4) of the 2006 Act is to be made, any issues relevant to that application; and

d. any other issue not going to the merits or fairness of the scheme, but which might lead the court to refuse to sanction the scheme."

At this first hearing the court will examine all the evidence presented to it, to include the composition of the various classes of creditors and/or members via the detailed information supplied, and any jurisdictional arguments. If satisfied with the proposal, the court will then order that the plan is voted on by those classes at a meeting and the Plan shall proceed to that stage.

Detailed relevant information in respect of the Plan, as set out in paragraph 7 of the Practice Statement will then be sent to every creditor or member who will be entitled to participate at the meeting. The concluding sentence of paragraph 7 states:

"It is the responsibility of the applicant to ensure that such notification is given in a concise form and is communicated to all persons affected by the scheme in the manner which is most appropriate to the circumstances of the case."

The rationale behind the Plan is that every creditor or member whose rights are affected by the compromise or arrangement shall be permitted to participate in the meeting (s.901C (3)). However, there is then a more sophisticated step to be carried out by s.901C (4), as the court can exclude, on application, a class of creditors or members of the company if it is satisfied that none of the members of the class has a "genuine economic interest" in the company. Clearly, therefore, before the meeting is held there may be an opportunity for the applicant to gain an advantage and steer on whether the Plan is likely to be successful. It will be interesting to see how this provision develops in practice as this remedy becomes more established, as it could promote disputes if the party to be excluded argues that the test of "genuine economic interest" is not satisfied. Presumably, valuation evidence will be crucial.

Assuming all goes as expected at the first hearing for the applicant company, the Plan will then need to be approved by the creditors or members and that will occur if 75% in value of the creditors or class of creditors or members or class of members (as the case may be) of those present and voting within each class vote in favour of the plan (s.901F (1)). However, note that this section is subject to the provisions in ss.901G and H. In essence, because of s.901G, there are still further opportunities for the Plan to be approved even if one or more classes is dissenting. This is known as the "cross-class cram down" procedure (see section 5 below).

This is materially different to the voting scheme for a Scheme of Arrangement, where, in addition to the 75% in value of those voting there is also a requirement for a majority in number of each class to vote in favour.

If the vote is successful, and the rules considered in section 5, for cross-class cram down are met, then the court will consider at a second hearing whether to sanction the plan and make it binding on all affected creditors or shareholders (s.901F). Just like the Scheme of Arrangement procedure, the court has absolute discretion to refuse to sanction the restructuring plan even if the restructuring plan was approved by the requisite amount of creditors. This shows the supremacy of the court in this process.

If, however, the Plan is sanctioned by the court, the restructuring plan is binding on all creditors and members when the Order is filed with the registrar of companies (s.901F (6)), or, for overseas companies, when the details are published in the Gazette.

What is the anticipated time period for this process? If the example of a scheme is followed, it is probable that the process will require at least six weeks from the date upon which application is made to the court for the first convening hearing. In addition, the secret of this procedure will clearly be all the preparatory work that is done with the relevant stakeholders, meaning that it could take even longer.

5. Cross-class cram down (s.901G)

As stated above, this is a new and powerful feature. Notwithstanding that a class does not reach the 75% threshold referred to above, the creditors in that class may be bound by the plan if the cross-class cram down rules are met. Those rules are that:

i.   at least one class of creditors or members who would receive a payment, or have a genuine economic interest in the company, in the event of the relevant alternative, voted in favour of the Plan (s.901G(5)); and

ii. the dissenting creditors would not be any worse off under that Plan than they would have be in the event of the relevant alternative (s.901G (3)).

"Relevant alternative" is defined in s.901G (4) as being what the court considers would be most likely to occur in relation to the company if the compromise or arrangement were not sanctioned as above under s.901F.

The premise of this provision is that there is an extra opportunity for the court to sanction the Plan through this process. In practice, it is presumably the case that the court will be utilising liquidation as the relevant alternative procedure. It is for this reason that the cross-class cram down is seen as a particularly powerful provision.

As with other areas of this Act, the Secretary of State has the ability to vary the conditions for cross-class cram down through the implementation of Regulations under the affirmative resolution procedure (s.901G(7)).

6. Interaction with the moratorium process

The court is given powers to make additional orders where a Plan for a company in liquidation or administration is sanctioned, such as, to bring the administration or liquidation to an end, to stay it, or to impose any requirements to facilitate the Plan as the court thinks fit. This is entirely logical and mirrors what is done if an administration order is granted by the court when a winding up petition is already in existence.

In addition, there are specific provisions in the Act where application for the Plan is made before the end of 12 weeks (beginning with the day after the end of the moratorium for the company). Now this may be quite rare, but it will be interesting to see if some innovative approaches are made by practitioners in this area. In this case, under s.901H (5), the court may not sanction the plan if creditors with a "moratorium debt" or a "priority pre-moratorium debt" are affected and have not agreed to it.

Such creditors, however, may not participate in the meeting summoned under s.901C described earlier in this chapter.

In this regard, it is important to cross refer to the references in Chapter 4 concerning debts arising as a result of the acceleration of loan agreements during the moratorium, and the change in their status that developed through the parliamentary process. These debts are <u>not</u> priority pre moratorium debts. This means that they can still be compromised without agreement as s.901H (5)) will not apply to them.

7. Conclusion

The Plan has the potential to be a powerful new remedy as it is clearly flexible and, as we have seen, binds all classes of creditors and even potentially dissenting classes. It will be interesting to see if practitioners use it in conjunction with the moratorium in the light of matters discussed in section 6 above or whether it works on a stand alone basis. The moratorium will of course potentially give the "breathing space" to undertake the necessary negotiations and preparatory work that are important in this process.

The academic and practical discussion of this new restructuring process has not been nearly as vocal as that surrounding the moratorium, which may not be surprising as the moratorium process is totally new.

One final consideration is whether this new Plan will be used in more than just large corporate restructurings. This is certainly the case with the existing Part 26 schemes. However, if the Plan is used in the SME market it could be a real alternative to the CVA procedure as it potentially has some distinct advantages over that process, and dissenting creditors could find that their voice is not as powerful because of the cross-class cram down provisions.

CHAPTER SIX
HOW SUPPLIERS AND CONTRACTORS ARE AFFECTED BY THE CORPORATE INSOLVENCY AND GOVERNANCE ACT 2020

1. Introduction

This is the third of the permanent insolvency changes brought in by the Act. It is potentially quite wide ranging, but it is not a new concept as somewhat lighter variations exist in earlier legislation.

Contractors and suppliers are fundamental to business. In almost every corporate insolvency there is a situation where such people or entities are owed monies and form part of the unsecured creditor group.

Nearly all commercial contracts include provisions which are known as "ipso facto" clauses. In simple terms, this is a term in a contract which enables one party to terminate the contract on the other party entering insolvency proceedings. How such clauses are drafted obviously varies depending on what is agreed between the parties and the relative bargaining strength at the time the contract is agreed. A termination clause of this nature is of vital importance for a supplier of goods and services, otherwise they may find that their debt continues to increase with no hope of payment.

On the other side of the equation, though, it may be very important to the company that is close to or has entered insolvency to keep a supply contract going, particularly if the company is contemplating administration or a company voluntary arrangement ("CVA") and wanting to continue trading. Therefore, a balancing act must be struck between two competing aims.

2. Background to the provisions

These are not completely new provisions but now much wider in scope than before. In 2015 there was the Insolvency (Protection of Essential Supplies) Order 2015 (SI 2015/989), which created a new s.233A into the Insolvency Act 1986.

This provided that, if a company entered administration or became subject to a CVA (not liquidation), an" ipso facto" term of a contract for the supply of "essential" goods or services would cease to have effect. The crucial point here is that it only applied to "essential" goods or services. In essence this only really caught utilities and IT supplies.

The provision was really a balancing act, as, the trade-off for this limitation for the suppliers was that they had the right to terminate, where post insolvency supply debts were not paid within 28 days of becoming due. Secondly, the supplier could insist upon a personal guarantee from the officeholder for post-insolvency charges and if the guarantee was not forthcoming then the supply could also be terminated.

As has been mentioned earlier in this book, there have been various recent consultations on the reform of corporate insolvency and this area of "ipso facto" clauses has been part of that debate. In the Department for Business, Energy & Industrial Strategy (BEIS) response to the latest consultation in 2018, it signalled its intention to introduce legislation to go further on the prevention of the enforcement of such clauses. The provisions created by the new Act do indeed go a lot further towards including all contracts for the supply of goods and services, with the clear objective of ensuring continuity of supplies for companies in financial difficulty and seeking to ensure, wherever possible, that the business can continue.

The Act is not limited only to new contracts and applies to any contract within the scope of the Act, even if that contract already existed before 26 June 2020.

As with other provisions in the Act, the Insolvency Service has published a fact sheet (which actually pre-dates the Act) and it can be found at:

https://www.gov.uk/government/publications/corporate-insolvency-and-governance-bill-2020-factsheets/prohibition-of-termination-clauses

3. Where to find the law

A new s.233B is introduced into the Insolvency Act 1986 by s.14 of the Act. It is entitled "Protection of supplies of goods and services". Further, s.233 (10) creates Sch.4ZZA which provides for exclusions from that section (found at Sch.12 in the Act, together with other consequential amendments). A new s.233C gives the Secretary of State the power by regulations to amend s.233B and Sch.4ZZA (a familiar theme in this Act). There is a temporary exclusion for "small suppliers" until 30th September 2020 created by s.15 of the Act. Finally, ss.16-19, together with Sch.13, create similar provisions under Northern Ireland legislation.

For ease of referencing going forward (as with other earlier referencing for the moratorium), references will be to the amended legislation in the Insolvency Act 1986.

4. Overview of the law

In summary, these new provisions complement and extend the existing ss.233 and 233A of the Insolvency Act 1986 by extending those restrictions to all kinds of suppliers, with the exception of "small suppliers" who have a temporary reprieve until 1st October 2020.

By s.233B (1) the provisions apply where a company becomes subject to a relevant insolvency procedure. Therefore, apart from administration, administrative receivership or a CVA it would also include liquidation and provisional liquidation. It also applies where a company becomes subject to the Act's two new procedures, namely the moratorium and restructuring plan. It does not apply where a company is subject to a scheme of arrangement.

The significant change from the existing s.233A is that it is not restricted to 'essential' goods and services, but applies generally to any contract for the supply of goods or services (s.233B(3)) in all types of contracts or agreements.

This section is wider than just prohibiting clauses allowing suppliers of goods or services to terminate because a relevant insolvency procedure has occurred, as it also includes the words "any other thing" in relation to their contracts.

"Any other thing" could include circumstances such as making it a pre-condition of ongoing supply that pre-insolvency arrears are paid, or increasing prices for ongoing supply and effectively holding the debtor company to ransom (s.233B(3)(a) and (b)). This is, thus, a very wide prohibition with severe consequences for the supplier. Indeed, s.233B (7) makes the post-insolvency ransom issue absolutely clear.

However, unfortunately perhaps for the supplier, it goes even further. By s.233B(4), the Act also prohibits the supplier from exercising any contractual entitlement to terminate the contract or supply because of an event occurring before the start of the insolvency period, where the entitlement has arisen before the start of that period. The breadth of this provision will be considered later in this chapter.

The insolvency period for the purposes of s.233B is set out in s.233B (8) as beginning when the company becomes subject to the relevant insolvency procedure, and ending at the times identified by reference to each individual procedure. We are used in the Act to the "relevant insolvency procedure" definition and then s.233B (8) sets out in subsections (a) – (g) how the test is applied for each of those procedures.

There are exceptions to this process set out in s.233B(5), whereby the supplier may still terminate the contract or exercise the entitlement during the insolvency procedure, if:

i.   The company or officeholder consents to the termination (s.233B(5)(a)) and (b); or

ii. The court is satisfied that the continuation of the contract would cause the supplier hardship, and grants permission for termination (s.233B (5) (c)).

If these conditions apply, then the supplier is entitled to terminate the contract in accordance with the contractual terms that exist between the parties. Also, by s.233B(6), a contract can also then be terminated if the company later becomes subject to a further relevant insolvency procedure by following the procedure set out in s.233B(5) (a)-(c).

As mentioned in section 3 above, it is s.233C that then gives the Secretary of State wide powers to amend any of these new provisions in s.233B and Sch.4ZZA.

5. What about existing rights – are they affected?

As indicated above, s.233B (4) confirms that termination of the contract after the occurrence of the insolvency trigger event is prohibited, if rights that arose before the relevant event have not been exercised. However, once the insolvency trigger event has occurred, suppliers will be able to terminate a contract on other contractual grounds, such as non-payment, or breach of contract. Accordingly, where a supplier has an entitlement to terminate the contract on a ground other than insolvency, and suspects an impending insolvency of one its clients, the supplier clearly needs to act swiftly.

6. Exceptions and Exclusions

The Act has both contractual and persons exceptions and exclusions. Some exceptions set out in ss.233B (5) and (6) have already been mentioned above. How the courts will interpret the "hardship" test in s.233B (5) (c) will no doubt evolve as case law develops.

There are also exclusions for those essential supplies which already fall within s. 233A (1), as they will continue to be governed by that regime (see Sch.4ZZA. Part 1).

Perhaps more significant are the "financial services" exclusions set out in Part 2 of Sch.4ZZA (paras 3 to 10).The excluded entities include insurers, banks, electronic money institutions, investment banks and investment firms, payment institutions, recognised investment exchanges or clearing houses, and securitisation companies. This seems to be a recognition by the Government that if the financial industry was not exempted then even more pressure may be placed on companies in difficulty. The net effect of this is that in practice the new provisions only really affect trade creditors in practice.

The exclusions also extend to any company or supplier functioning outside the United Kingdom, providing that the relevant activities would bring it within the Sch.4ZZA Part 1 exclusions if they been undertaken in the UK.

Next are the financial services contracts exclusions as set out in Sch.4ZZA, Part 3 and the financial markets exclusions in Part 4.

It is worth noting that if, through the insolvency process, a business is transferred into a 'Newco' structure, perhaps through an administration sale, then there is no ongoing obligation on the supplier to supply the Newco.

Finally, there is a temporary exclusion for "small" company suppliers. This will apply until 30 September 2020 (as defined in s.15 of the Act). It will be interesting to see if this period is extended.

There are financial and other conditions to qualify for this exclusion as set out in s.15 (4)-(10) of the Act. In essence, these are based on the most recent financial year and are:

i.   turnover not more than £10.2 million;

ii. balance sheet total not more than £5.1 million; and

iii. employees not more than 50.

(There are modifications in relation to suppliers in their first financial year of trading).

7. Conclusion

These supply provisions are quite lengthy and will need to be subject to detailed examination. They are likely to have a significant impact on suppliers, and they will have to review their procedures carefully. Legal advisors need to be aware of these changes on behalf of their clients, and should advise all their commercial clients to review their supply terms and consider redrafting where necessary to protect against the consequences of an insolvency event occurring. It is anticipated that wider pre-insolvency triggers of default will be seen (non-payment on its own will, of course, not bring these provisions into play).

Above all, this will put increasing importance on financial and credit monitoring, and the ability to identify early warning signs of company difficulty.

CHAPTER SEVEN
WRONGFUL TRADING AND DIRECTORS' DUTIES GENERALLY UNDER THE CORPORATE INSOLVENCY AND GOVERNANCE ACT 2020

1. Introduction

Having analysed the permanent reforms set out in the Act in the earlier chapters, we now turn to two temporary reforms in this and the following chapter. However, as we have seen, there were also some temporary provisions within the permanent reforms to take account of the current COVID-19 pandemic. This is particularly in the moratorium process. The first of these temporary changes is described as the suspension of wrongful trading. That is actually a rather simplistic statement, as will be seen below.

The clear thinking behind this is to enable directors of companies which are affected by the pandemic to be free to make decisions about the future of their company, without the threat of becoming liable to personally contribute to the company's assets if insolvency then follows. It is, thus, another of the economic support measures for companies.

In order to understand these changes it is necessary first to analyse the law as it existed for wrongful trading before the Act was born.

2. The law pre the Act

It is well established law that where a company is trading profitably, the directors carry out their duties for the benefit of the company and its shareholders.

However, this set of duties changes when the company is either insolvent or at serious risk of insolvency. Then, under s.172 of the Companies Act 2006, their overriding responsibility is to act in the best interests of the creditors of the company.

Following this change of emphasis, a director may be liable for wrongful trading under s.214 and s.246ZB of the IA 1986 and risk personal liability. A wrongful trading action may be brought by a liquidator only after the company has gone into insolvent liquidation, or (from 1 October 2015) by an administrator where the company has gone into insolvent administration.

If at some time before the winding up or administration, the director knew, or ought to have known, that there was no reasonable prospect that the company would avoid insolvent liquidation or administration, the director may be found guilty of wrongful trading and have to make a contribution to the company's assets.

All directors are therefore expected to show some level of financial understanding and diligence, and take advice if their company is in financial difficulties.

When looking at whether a director knew, or ought to have known, that the company could not avoid insolvent liquidation or administration, both subjective and objective tests are applied (IA 1986, s.214 (4)). That is:

a) What did this particular director know?

b) And what would a reasonable director have known in the circumstances?

Matters such as the size of the business, the director's function (e.g., a finance director is expected to have a greater degree of competence on accountancy matters than other directors), are looked at. In practice, the insolvency practitioner will seek clear evidence of insolvency about which any director should have been aware. Some examples could be:

a) insolvency on a balance sheet basis;

b) creditor pressure;

c) late filing of accounts;

d) any qualification on the accounts by the auditors;

e) the practice of paying the creditors only when they issue proceedings or statutory demands; or

f) numerous judgments against the company.

That is not the full story, however, as s.214 (3) of the IA 1986 provides a defence for the director. This is that the director took every step with a view to minimise a potential loss to the company's creditors, after he became aware that the company had no prospects of avoiding insolvent liquidation or administration. This could potentially include taking professional advice, both legal and accountancy; minimising further goods taken on credit; effective collection of debts, and drawing up frequent management accounts (possibly daily) to establish the financial position of the company.

If wrongful trading is established, a director may be ordered to make a personal contribution for the loss that he has caused by his actions. The section establishes that the personal contribution is compensatory rather than punitive.

On a personal level, precautions that a director may wish to take to protect him or herself from an accusation of wrongful trading could include:

a) keeping an accurate record of his or her own activities, including board meetings;

b) being satisfied that the financial records kept are sufficient;

c) seeking professional advice at the earliest sign of financial problems in the company;

d) raising with the board financial concerns when these start to become evident; and

e) possibly resigning (but resignation does not provide an absolute defence).

A case considering this area was *Singla v Hedman, Gone to Hell Limited & Stonewood Communications BV (2010) EWHC 902 (Ch)*.

More recent cases have been firstly *Re Ralls Builders Ltd (in liquidation); Grant and another (Joint Liquidators of Ralls Builders Ltd) v Ralls and others (2016)EWHC 243 (Ch)*, with an interesting subsequent costs judgment from this case on this area at *(2016) EWHC 1812 (Ch)*. Secondly, the case of *Brooks* and *another v Armstrong and another (2015) EWHC 2289 (Ch)*, was decided in favour of the directors at first instance before Mr Registrar Jones. Interestingly, the liquidators and the directors both appealed the judgment which was heard before David Foxton QC, sitting as a Deputy Judge of the High Court, *(2016) EWHC 2893 (Ch)*. On that appeal, the liquidator was not successful. Finally, the case of *Nicholson v Fielding [2017] All ER (D) 156 (Oct)*, also saw the liquidator being defeated.

In each of these cases, the insolvency practitioner was unsuccessful, with appropriate costs consequences following. It is fair to say that wrongful trading cases being pursued to trial in recent times following these cases have reduced, with insolvency practitioners being more cautious. Of course, the remedy is threatened in many cases by either the liquidator or the administrator in order to seek to obtain negotiated financial settlements against directors.

3. The new temporary provisions

Having set the provisions in context above, what are the changes brought in by the Act?

The relevant provision is set out in s.12 for Great Britain and is entitled "Suspension of liability for wrongful trading". The corresponding Northern Ireland provision is found in s.13. There are not any major Schedules which relate to this provision, although references are made in the Great Britain legislation to Sch.ZA1 of the IA 1986 (set out in Sch.1 of the Act).

As with other provisions in the Act, the Insolvency Service has published a fact sheet (which pre-dates the Act) and it can be found at:

https://www.gov.uk/government/publications/corporate-insolvency-and-governance-bill-2020-factsheets/suspension-of-wrongful-trading-liability

This measure extends to the whole of the United Kingdom, commenced retrospectively from 1ˢᵗ March 2020 and is due to expire on

30th September 2020. There is a power for the Government via secondary legislation to extend this for a further period of up to six months, if it considers it to be necessary and appropriate. This will presumably be exercised if the economic effects of the pandemic are continuing.

These sections describe a temporary change in the law surrounding liability for wrongful trading for company directors so they can keep their businesses going without the threat of personal liability.

However, it is actually rather too simplistic to say that there is a temporary suspension of wrongful trading. What the Act actually does is specify that, in determining the contribution to a company's assets that it is proper for a person to make, the court is to <u>assume</u> that the person is not responsible for any worsening of the financial position of the company or its creditors that occurs during the period this provision is in operation (s.12 (1)).

In theory, the word "assume", must leave open the possibility that a different conclusion could be reached by the court if the evidence is clear that the directors have indeed been responsible for the worsening of the financial position and so the presumption is rebutted.

Finally, unlike some of the provisions we shall consider in the next chapter surrounding winding up petitions, there is no requirement here to show that the company's worsening financial position was due exclusively, or in part, to the COVID-19 situation.

4. Exclusions

As with other provisions in the Act, the wrongful trading suspension sections do not apply to many financial services firms and public-private partnership project companies. This is the effect of ss.12 (3) and (4) and then s.12 (6) also excludes any company carrying out a regulated activity under s.4A of the Financial Services and Markets Act 2000 and is not subject to a requirement imposed by that Act to refrain from holding money for clients.

It is also interesting that there does not appear to be any similar temporary provision that applies to Limited Liability Partnerships ("LLPs"). By s.214A of the IA 1986, a person who has been a member and who has taken drawings during the two years prior to insolvency may be ordered by the court to make repayment, if at the time of the withdrawal the LLP was unable to pay its debts (within the meaning of Section 123 of the IA 1986) or would become unable to pay its debts after withdrawal. For repayment to be ordered the court also has to be satisfied that after each withdrawal the member knew or ought to have concluded that there was no reasonable prospect that the limited liability partnership would avoid going into insolvent liquidation.

Thus, it seems that the law relating to clawbacks in LLPs remains as it always has since s.214A of the IA 1986 was brought into force.

5. What about other potential director offences?

This "suspension" only relates to the wrongful trading provisions and so all other potential offences remain in play. A director could still find him or herself liable for fraudulent trading (although this is a more difficult claim to pursue), or misfeasance. Directors could also face director disqualification proceedings (and so a potential compensation order under the provisions that came into force in 2015 via the Small Business, Enterprise and Employment Act 2015). In addition, none of the antecedent transaction provisions (transactions at an undervalue; preferences; transactions to defraud creditors and illegal dividends) are suspended either.

All the duties of directors, as seen in ss.171 to 177 of the Companies Act 2006, will also still apply. These include promoting the success of the company, exercising independent judgment and exercising reasonable care, skill and diligence.

So, the onus is still on a director to act sensibly, take professional advice where necessary and keep accurate written records of all decisions. Technically, one could imagine a situation where a court has found that wrongful trading has occurred but will not ask the directors to contribute to the company's assets as a consequence because of this temporary suspension provision. However, this would be a significant finding if other offences are being pursued.

6. Conclusion

As the recent cases considered earlier in this chapter have shown, wrongful trading already had a relatively high barrier of proof and was not actively pursued to trial by liquidators or administrators. In practice, therefore, it may be that this temporary change will not make any real difference in practice.

However, lawyers and other professionals should still be clear in their advice to directors that they must continue to act properly and with careful reference to their overarching duties.

CHAPTER EIGHT
STATUTORY DEMANDS, WINDING UP PETITIONS AND ORDERS UNDER THE CORPORATE INSOLVENCY AND GOVERNANCE ACT 2020

1. Introduction

The second of these temporary changes surround areas that are well known to lawyers working in this area as they are crucial parts of the compulsory liquidation process. Once again, the thinking behind these measures is to provide economic support for companies but for a time limited period.

Just as with the previous chapter, in order to understand these changes it is necessary first to analyse the law as it existed in this area before the Act came into force.

2. The law pre the Act

The test for insolvency used for most corporate insolvency procedures is well established and contained in ss. 122 and 123 IA 1986, and is based on the company's ability or otherwise to pay its debts.

A company is deemed unable to pay its debts if:

(a) a creditor owed more than £750 has served a formal written demand on the company (a 'statutory demand'), waited three weeks and has not been paid or come to an arrangement with the company (s. 123(1) (a)) or;

(b) in England and Wales, a creditor has obtained judgment against the company *and* attempted to execute the judgment (by sending court officials to recover assets or cash from the company), and the debt is still unsatisfied in full or in part (s. 123(1)(b)) or;

(c) in Scotland, the induciae of a charge for payment on an extract decree, or an extract registered bond, or an extract registered protest, have expired without payment being made (s.123(1)(c)) or

(d) if, in Northern Ireland, a certificate of unenforceability has been granted in respect of a judgment against the company (s.123(1)(d)) or

(e) it can be proved to the court that the company cannot pay its debts as they fall due (often known as the 'cash flow test') (s. 123(1)(e); or

(f) it can be proved to the court that the company's assets are less than its liabilities (often known as the 'balance sheet test') (s. 123(2).

In practice, options for an unsecured creditor who is owed money are either (a)to serve a statutory demand for a debt in excess of £750 (s.123(1)(a)), then to wait three weeks before presenting a petition to the court to put the company into liquidation or(b) to take conventional debt legal proceedings against the company; obtain judgment; attempt to execute the judgment (s. 123 (1) (b)) and then, if that execution process is unsatisfied, present a petition to the court to put the company into liquidation.

A statutory demand or petition itself can, of course, be defended by the debtor company and injunctions can be applied for to stop further action. At such a hearing, the court will consider all relevant factors, and may dismiss the statutory demand or petition if the debtor company can show that it may recover its financial position, or if the debt is disputed in any way by the debtor company. There have been many cases considering the relevant tests to be applied here. The Court of Appeal set out the relevant law in this area in the case of *Tallington Lakes Ltd v Ancasta International Boat Sales Ltd [2012] EWCA Civ 1712*. In general terms, if the debtor company is able to establish a genuine and substantial dispute, the petitioning creditor will be injuncted and prevented from proceeding with the petition. For a recent case on this area, see *LDX International Group LLP v Misra Ventures Ltd [2018] EWHC 275(Ch)*. There are some very limited exceptions to this, for example, *Lacontha Foundation v GBI Investments Limited [2010] EWHC 37 (Ch)*, in which the High Court set out guidelines for assessing whether the winding up order should be made, even when the debt is disputed. Of course, if the petitioning creditor has a judgment already, it will be very difficult for the debtor company to succeed in arguing that there is a dispute unless it is also able to have the judgment set aside.

If the winding up petition is accepted and the winding-up order is made, the Official Receiver ("OR"), a civil servant and court official employed by the Insolvency Service, will automatically become liquidator. The OR must decide whether it is appropriate for the creditors to appoint an insolvency practitioner as liquidator in their place, either directly through the Secretary of State powers that the OR has, or upon receipt of a request from a majority of creditors. Obviously, no private practice insolvency practitioner will be willing to act unless there are sufficient assets within the company to pay their fees.

3. Background and overview of the new temporary provisions

Having set the existing legal position in context above, albeit briefly, what are the temporary changes brought in by the Act?

Firstly, the background to these changes was trailed by the Government in an announcement on 23 April 2020 with the reason being given that it was to "safeguard the UK high street against aggressive debt recovery actions" during the COVID-19 crisis. The problems in the retail sector have been well documented in recent years.

However, the provisions that came into force are much wider than simply protecting commercial tenants in the retail sector, and are applicable across the whole of the winding up regime for any debt.

The relevant law is set out in s.10 of the Act for Great Britain. The similar Northern Ireland provision is found in s.11. Sch.10 and Sch. 11, respectively, contain the details of the temporary provisions. Because they are temporary provisions, although reference is obviously made to the IA 1986, these changes stand alone via this Act. Again, there are provisions giving the Secretary of State the power to extend this period for a further 6 months (see s.41 of the Act).

It is also important to read these provisions together with linked Practice Directions. Reference has been made earlier in this book to a temporary Practice Direction that was issued with effect from 6th April 2020 to provide solutions, for court users, to the problems that were arising very swiftly as soon as the pandemic problems began affecting litigation procedure. A number of the measures were created to alleviate the problems caused by courts not being open. It was stated that the temporary Practice Direction would remain in force until 1st October 2020, unless amended or revoked by a subsequent Practice Direction. A formal new Practice Direction was then issued in June and titled: "Insolvency Practice Direction relating to the Corporate Insolvency and Governance Act 2020".

This document can be found at:

https://www.judiciary.uk/wp-content/uploads/2020/07/Insolvency-Practice-Direction-relating-to-the-Corporate-Insolvency-and-Governance-Act-2020.pdf

It takes effect from the 26th June 2020, the same date as the commencement of the Act, and is required reading for all who practice in this area. Although it is right to refer to it in this Chapter, because a number of the provisions relate to winding up petitions issued on or before 30th September 2020, other provisions of the Act are also referred to.

These provisions are very wide ranging and apply to a registered company; any foreign company or other association or entity which could be wound up by our courts under the normal IA 1986 provisions and the winding up of an insolvent partnership.. Of course, individual partners in an insolvent partnership can still be subject to bankruptcy proceedings. For the avoidance of doubt, this Act does not include any restrictions on personal insolvency creditor actions.

Finally, as with other provisions in the Act, the Insolvency Service has published a fact sheet (which again predates the Act) which can be found at:

https://www.gov.uk/government/publications/corporate-insolvency-and-governance-bill-2020-factsheets/statutory-demands-and-winding-up-notices

4. Analysis of the separate provisions

i. Temporary Absolute Ban on Statutory Demands

There is an absolute ban on statutory demands being used for presenting winding up petitions for any debt whatsoever. Statutory demands served between 1 March 2020 and 30 September 2020 cannot form the basis of a winding up petition presented at any point after 27 April 2020 (Sch.10, paras 1(1)-(4)).

That does not mean that an alternative formal demand for non-payment of monies owed cannot be made, but it may be a toothless action in reality Following that through, even though a statutory demand could still be served, any debtor company will know that it then can't be taken further with the issue of a winding up petition. It may be a threat that some creditors wish to make, but a well advised debtor company will simply ignore it.

ii. The effect on Winding up Petitions

Unlike statutory demands, these are not totally prevented in law, but the reality in practice is that they really are, because of the way the provisions are drafted.

By Sch.10, paras 2-3, creditors should not present a petition between the period 27th April to 30th September 2020 unless they are satisfied that either:

i. coronavirus hasn't had a financial effect on the debtor company; or

ii. the company would have been unable to pay its debts regardless of coronavirus.

Petitioning creditors must make a statement to this effect in the petition.

The consequences of this provision is that if a winding up petition is actually presented and the court finds that the conditions above are not satisfied, then the petition will be dismissed with potential costs risks for the petitioning creditor to being held liable for the debtor company's legal costs.

The aforesaid Practice Direction gives further detail on what the petitioning creditor has to do to seek to convince the court that these hurdles can be overcome.

In practice, the commercial advice for clients wanting to go down this route must be to be very careful, as the court is presumably going to be reticent in allowing a petition to proceed if there is any evidence at all of the coronavirus having a financial effect on the company. Presumably, if this temporary period is not extended, a creditor could wait until after 30th September 2020 to start the process and may have a greater chance of succeeding.

The few cases that were seen before the Act commenced, but after the provisions had been announced in broad terms or seen in the Bill, tend to support the view that the petitioning creditor will have an uphill struggle (see section 5 below).

Because these provisions were trailed before the Act came into force, Sch.10, para 4 covers the position of winding up petitions issued on or after 27th April but before the 26th June, and creates similar hurdles.

iii When can a winding-up order be made?

Even if the petitioning creditor overcomes the above tests and the petition is allowed to proceed, that is not the end of the process.

A winding up order may only be made if the court is satisfied that the company would be unable to pay its debts even if the coronavirus had not had a financial effect on the company (see Sch.10 paras 5-6). In essence, then, there may be a further opportunity for the debtor company to escape the order.

iv Orders made between 27th April 2020 and 25th June 2020

Sch.10, para 7 covers the situation where a winding up order is made before the commencement of the Act but on or after 27th April 2020. In such cases, the court is regarded as having no power to make the order and so it is void, on the basis that it does not meet the new requirements for the making of an order as set out in Sch.10, paras 5-6 above.

By Sch.10, para 7(4) the court can give directions to the OR, liquidator or provisional liquidator as it thinks fit for the purpose of restoring the company to the position it was in immediately before the petition was presented. Presumably, though, the petitioning creditor would not face costs orders as that would seem inequitable.

5. Case law

It is not surprising that there were several cases around this area which came to court in that interim period when the legislation had been announced in general terms or was in draft form) but before the Act came into force.

These included cases where the courts have considered whether to restrain the presentation or advertisement of winding up petitions in light of the impending legislation.

In *Shorts Gardens LLP v Camden London Borough Council [2020] EWHC 1001*, the Judge was aware of an announcement by the Government of these pending changes due to press releases, but draft legislation was not before him. In that case, the petitioning creditor was allowed to proceed, but the case was decided very much on its own facts. *Travelodge Hotels Ltd v Prime Aesthetics Ltd and others [2020] EWHC 1217 (Ch)* was also decided in the same time period but in this case the petitioner was not allowed to proceed with his action.

The cases of R*e A Company [2020] EWHC 1406* and *Re A Company [2020] EWHC 1551*, were decided after the Corporate Insolvency and Governance Bill had been published, but prior to it receiving Royal Assent. In the first case, Mr Justice Morgan granted an urgent *ex parte* application to restrain the presentation of a winding up petition by a landlord of a high street retailer. In the second case, the court restrained advertisement of a petition in relation to a very aged debt, as the petitioner had not provided sufficient evidence to satisfy the court that the company would have been unable to pay its debts regardless of the financial effects of the coronavirus.

These cases are not binding in any way now the legislation is in force, but they may be of persuasive consideration.

6. The interaction with s.127 IA 1986 and the linked consequences

Sch.10, para 9 is a very interesting provision which has perhaps not received the attention it deserves. It provides for the purposes of s.129 IA 1986, that the commencement of the winding-up will be the date of the order rather than the date of presentation of the petition. Effectively, this is rendering useless the normally powerful provision in s.127 IA 1986 (dispositions of property between the date of the presentation of the petition and the order itself being normally void unless validation orders are obtained). Following that through, validation orders will not now be required during the period of these temporary provisions.

(See earlier chapters for reference to s.127 IA 1986 and its operation in the context of the moratorium).

Sch.10, paras 10-18 then flow from this position by changing the various provisions which rely on the "onset of insolvency" and creating some modifications to the IA 1986. These are very detailed and require careful analysis, but in normal times these provisions concern transactions at an undervalue and preferences and highlight that the trigger point of the onset of insolvency is very important.

By Sch.10, para 15 the time provisions are varied whilst these provisions remain in force. The relevant period is now to start either (a) 2 years before the date of presentation of the petition (in the case of transactions at an undervalue) or six months (in the case of preferences) or (and here is the significant change) (b) 2½ years before the day on which the winding-up order was made (in the case of transactions at an undervalue) or 12 months (in the case of preferences) whichever is the later, ending with the day on which the winding-up order is made.

7. Conclusion

On the basis that creditors err on the side of caution because of these temporary provisions, we can expect compulsory petition numbers to continue to decline. According to the statistics published by the Insolvency Service, in June 2020 there were only 61 orders made. But, of course, debts will potentially continue to accrue and these provisions may simply be delaying future problems? Alternatively, will companies make use of alternative rescue provisions in the Act or the original insolvency legislation?

Finally, by way of completeness, a series of other debt enforcement preventative measures were also brought into force by secondary legislation so Bailiffs and High Court Enforcement Officers have had to get used to those and advise their clients accordingly. Again, some of these measures have caused concern for commercial landlords who have felt that their options were being very much limited.

CHAPTER NINE
COMPANY FILINGS UNDER THE CORPORATE INSOLVENCY AND GOVERNANCE ACT 2020

1. Introduction

Whereas the bulk of the Act covers provisions that are relevant to the insolvency and restructuring practitioner, there are also some other administrative relaxations included on a temporary basis and, for the sake of completeness, these are set out briefly in this chapter. In simple terms, these relate to the holding of meetings and the various statutory filings that companies are required to undertake with Companies House. Given the potential difficulties caused by the pandemic, it is right that changes have been made. Under existing law there are financial penalties for a failure to complete filings, and potential criminal liability too, so these provisions again relax the pressure on directors and company secretaries. Companies House has also very helpfully expanded its procedures for the uploading of certain documents online that would usually be sent in a paper format. However, only limited companies and limited liability partnerships ("LLPs") are able to use this service.

Returning to the insolvency profession, practitioners also have many filing duties in corporate insolvency so it is important for them to also be aware of these provisions.

Again, the Insolvency Service has published fact sheets (which as with the earlier ones referred to in this book, predate the Act) which can be found at:

https://www.gov.uk/government/publications/corporate-insolvency-and-governance-bill-2020-factsheets/annual-general-meetings-and-other-general-meetings

and

https://www.gov.uk/government/publications/corporate-insolvency-and-governance-bill-2020-factsheets/companies-house-filings

2. Where to find the law

The relevant provisions are found in ss.37-40 of the Act and Sch. 14.

These relaxations are backdated, so as to apply to any meeting or filings required from 26th March until 30th September. Whilst the current period of extension ends on 30th September, the Act allows for regulations to extend the period of providing information to the Registrar of Companies further up until a final date of 5th April 2021 (s.39).

Indeed, related regulations, namely the Companies etc. (Filing Requirements) (Temporary Modifications) Regulations 2020 (SI 2020 No. 645) ("the 2020 Regulations") have already come into force (on 27 June 2020) to exercise the relevant powers in the Companies Act 2006 and s.39 (1) and (4) of the Act and relax filing requirements.

These regulations can be found at:

https://www.legislation.gov.uk/uksi/2020/645/made/data.pdf

3. The substantive provisions

The Act assists in two areas around Annual General Meetings ("AGM") during this time. Firstly, it allows an extension to the period for holding the AGM. Secondly, it allows companies to hold a "closed" AGM.

(i) Extending the period in which a company must hold its AGM

By s.38 of the Act, if a public company (or any of the other entities referred to) is required to hold an AGM in a period ending at some point between 26 March and 30 September, the Act provides that the company can instead hold its AGM by 30 September, or on the last day of the period of 12 months immediately following the end of the relevant accounting period, if that is earlier than the 30th September. Company secretaries and advisors are well advised to calculate the final date carefully.

(ii) Holding a closed AGM or other meeting

In essence, the provisions set out in Sch.14 allow for any company that is legally required to hold AGMs ((and indeed General Meetings) to hold them virtually or by other means to avoid a face to face meeting. This is a straight response to the restrictions on public gatherings that have been in place since the beginning of the lockdown period. Shareholders still retain their right to vote at any such meeting, but they do not have the right to attend in person, or to participate beyond voting or to vote by any particular means.

These provisions will take precedence over any contradicting provisions in a company's Articles of Association.

Specifically to help companies consider how best to act in light of these new provisions, both the Department for Business, Energy &

Industrial Strategy (BEIS) and the Financial Reporting Council (FRC)(which is to be replaced by the Audit, Reporting and Governance Authority)have published guidance on best practice for holding AGMs. This was actually published about the same time as the Bill was first promulgated, but it still provides useful assistance and can be found here:

https://www.frc.org.uk/getattachment/e3224310-c39c-4b48-b56b-cc703936beeb/Updated-QA-AGMs-Best-Practice-Final.pdf

4. The 2020 Regulations

These apply to virtually all companies covered by the Companies Act 2006 and also limited partnerships (including Scottish ones), limited liability partnerships, unregistered companies, overseas companies and other European entities which have a duty to file documents or notices with Companies House.

Perhaps the most effective way of ensuring compliance with these requirements and regulations is to refer to the helpful guidance published on 1st July 2020 by Companies House which can be found here:

https://www.gov.uk/government/publications/the-companies-etc-filing-requirements-temporary-modifications-regulations-2020/temporary-changes-to-companies-house-filing-requirements

Affected filings include the ones that are seen most regularly in company law, namely accounts filings; the confirmation statement; changes to the company (for example, new or resigning directors, persons of significant control changes or articles alterations); and security and borrowing changes.

A careful reading of the regulations is required as various options and permutations do exist but some key provisions are highlighted below:

i.   accounts filing deadlines are generally extended by 3 months, to 12 months for private companies and 9 months for public companies.

ii. The 14 day deadline for the annual confirmation statement is extended to 42 days.

iii. The 14 day deadlines for submitting notices of company event changes (e.g. new directors or persons of significant control) are also extended to 42 days.

iv. The important 21 day deadline for registering a charge against a company's assets is extended by 10 days to 31 days. As is well known, the consequences of non-registration are potentially very serious indeed for the lender.

These temporary extensions apply if an entity's filing deadline falls on or after 27 June 2020 and until 5 April 2021. Entities with a filing deadline falling on or after 6 April 2021 will not receive an automatic extension, so, again, careful administration must be undertaken.

5. Conclusion

To a large extent these provisions are not controversial and should be welcomed as positive by companies and other entities. Practical and proactive advice could also be given by corporate and commercial lawyers as to whether adopting some of these provisions could be considered on a longer term basis by their clients. The current digital agenda does, of course, chime well with many of these changes. On the other hand, one big concern is the potential for these changes to reduce shareholder involvement, resulting in shareholders feeling disenfranchised at a time when many companies are clearly needing the support of their members.

CHAPTER TEN
FURTHER CHANGES ON
THE HORIZON?

1 Introduction

With so much focus on the Corporate Insolvency and Governance Act over recent months, it is tempting to think that it is the be all and end all of insolvency and restructuring reform. This certainly is not the case, however. Therefore, this final chapter will look at other areas of potential (or actual) reform in the profession and seek to prepare practitioners for them by summarising the main topics. The emphasis throughout this book has been on corporate insolvency, but it is important to remember that May 2021 will see the commencement of the much debated "Breathing Space" scheme for personal insolvency to be followed by the development of the Statutory Debt Repayment Plan. These will, no doubt, be the subject of much debate and discussion over the coming months.

This final chapter is also an apt time to remind all who work in this arena of the point made in the introductory chapter that, probably soon after this book is published, case law on the Act will begin to be made and more regulations may be published. Consequently, it is absolutely vital that all insolvency professionals keep themselves up to date. Indeed, as demonstrated in Chapter 8 (which analysed the temporary provisions around statutory demands and winding up petitions and orders), some cases were decided between the announcement of the proposed Bill and its enactment.

In no particular order, here are some actual and potential areas of change and reform.

2   The Administration process, to include Pre-Packaged Administrations

With the bringing into force of the moratorium process, there has been academic comment on whether it would be used as an alternative or a pre-curser to administration. Certainly, it promotes a similar breathing space. However, it is necessary to consider the administration process separately in terms of potential changes.

After the pandemic crisis began, two high profile companies went into administration, namely Debenhams and Carluccios. Both companies occupied many column inches in the business press over their financial struggles and both cases generated interesting case law around the interplay of employment law and administration in the context of furloughed employees.

The first instance decisions can be found at:

- *Re Carluccio's Limited (in administration) [2020] EWHC 88D (Ch).*

- *Re Debenhams Retail Ltd [2020] EWHC 921 (Ch).*

Both decisions reached the same conclusion on adoption of employment contracts for furloughed employees in administration. The Debenhams decision was then appealed to the Court of Appeal by the joint administrators and that judgment (upholding the first instance decision) can be found at:

Re Debenhams Retail Limited (In Administration) [2020] EWCA Civ. 600

Therefore, based on Court of Appeal authority it is now confirmed that, by accessing the Job Retention Scheme and paying employees on a furloughed basis, administrators have adopted the contracts of furloughed employees. The Court of Appeal recognised that this could result in a difficult situation for administrators and the rescue profession generally, but wanted Parliament's view as they felt bound by the law as it currently stood.

The somewhat unhappy relationship between employment law and insolvency law has been a regular theme over recent years through a number of well-known cases. We can expect further judicial interpretation in this field in the future, and all insolvency professionals need to be aware of the importance of taking specialist employment law advice if any rescue process is being considered where there is a significant number of employees potentially affected.

Of course, this issue has been seen often in pre-packaged administrations, and there is one important reference to that process in the Act. There was a "sunset clause" that existed via the Small Business Enterprise and Employment Act 2015 which expired in May 2020. This gave the Secretary of State, amongst other things, the power to make it a requirement that pre-packaged administration transactions with "connected" parties (often the directors of the failing company of course) be referred by these parties to an independent business entity (called the pre pack pool) for approval prior to completion. This power is voluntary at present with no sanctions for non-compliance, and is not often utilised by the company wishing to sell its business in this way. By s.8 of the Act, the ability for the Secretary of State to make an absolute provision to prohibit or impose requirements on the disposals of property to connected parties via pre-packaged administration is revived but these must now be used before the end of June 2021. Whether the extension will result in substantial changes in the process remains to be seen, but the opportunity is there.

Practitioners will also be very familiar with the problems caused in recent years surrounding out of hours filings to commence the administration process. Perhaps to prevent similar problems for the moratorium, there is a clear provision (paragraph 10) in the new Practice Direction of 2nd July, referred to earlier in this book, stating that where directors of a company file relevant documents with the court by means of electronic delivery for the purposes of obtaining a moratorium pursuant to s.A3 of the Act, the documents shall be treated as being filed with the court at the date and time recorded in the court email. This email is generated by automatic notification acknowledging that the documents have been submitted to the court. This follows the procedure laid down in Practice Direction 51O (The Electronic Working Pilot Scheme).

Finally on administrations, and returning to Debenhams, this is a case that is being dubbed a "light touch administration" as once the administrators were appointed, they let the senior management team continue to run the company. This has historically been quite unusual for an administration process. In a sense it brings an administration closer to the moratorium or company voluntary arrangement process where the directors remain in day to day control. Again, it illustrates the ever-developing law in this area and the potential interplay between the different rescue procedures.

3   HMRC regains preferential creditor status

This is a potentially important change and not one that has been welcomed by the profession. Legislation will be introduced on the 1st December 2020 via the Finance Act 2020, which received Royal Assent on 22nd July 2020. This will mean that HMRC will regain its preferential status in an administration and liquidation. HMRC is currently an unsecured creditor, after its previous preferential status was removed by the Enterprise Act 2002.

The result of this is that in these insolvent situations, HMRC will move up the ranking in terms of payment. Preferential debts are paid after fixed charges and the expenses of the insolvency practitioner, but before the holders of floating charges and all other unsecured creditors.

Under current rules, employees and the Financial Services Compensation Scheme ("FSCS") are the only preferential creditors in an insolvency situation. However, by this legislation, from 1st December, HMRC will join the FSCS as a secondary preferential creditor in relation to certain outstanding taxes to be paid by employees and customers that are held by a business. Employees will still rank before them. These taxes include PAYE, VAT, employee NICs and Construction Industry Scheme (CIS) deductions.

HMRC will continue to be an unsecured creditor for corporation tax and any other taxes owed directly by a company. The legislation as drafted does not include any restriction on the age of tax debts which can have preferential status.

Clearly this could have a significant effect on the dividends available for unsecured creditors, but it may also affect how lenders look at their commitment to businesses and they may seek extra security to protect their position going forward.

4   The Ethics Code for Insolvency Practitioners

This Code was updated and republished in May 2020, and has perhaps been overshadowed by the Act. A full analysis is outside the scope of this book. The two main Recognised Professional Bodies in England and Wales have each published their versions.

The Institute of Chartered Accountants in England and Wales ("ICAEW") version of the new Code can be found at:

www.icaew.com/-/media/corporate/files/technical/ethics/insolvency-code-of-ethics.ashx?la=en

The Insolvency Practitioners Association ("IPA") version of the new Code is at:

www.insolvency-practitioners.org.uk/regulation-and-guidance/ethics-code

The Joint Insolvency Committee concluded its consultation on a draft revised guide in July 2017, so this new publication has been a long time coming. It is required reading for all insolvency practitioners and their advisors. The overarching fundamental principles and framework remain the same as the former Code, but there is much more detail.

There are 5 fundamental principles, the spirit of which must always be complied with:

- Integrity

- Objectivity

- Professional competence and due care

- Confidentiality

- Professional Behaviour

In an age of increased spotlight on all professionals, it is important that a full understanding of this Code is obtained.

5   Regulation

This area follows closely from the Code of Ethics and again demonstrates that it is an area that will potentially develop in the next 12 months. There was a call for evidence on insolvency practitioner regulation published on 12th July 2019 which can found at:

https://assets.publishing.service.gov.uk/government/uploads/system/
uploads/attachment_data/file/816560/
Call_for_Evidence_Final_Proofed_Versionrev.pdf

Due to the very important and detailed work on the Act, the next stage in the process has not yet taken place but is expected later in 2020. This would be to explore whether the system of regulation is working satisfactorily or whether there is a need to make further changes, including whether to consult on a move to a single regulator. Regulation could be a very significant part of the agenda for the profession in the next 12 months.

6   Statements of Insolvency Practice ("SIPs")

These are issued to insolvency practitioners by their Recognised Professional Bodies to promote and maintain the standards of the profession. They are not laid down by Parliament but a breach of them could result in a practitioner facing disciplinary proceedings. There are currently 15 SIPs and they each relate to a particular area of insolvency practice. They are regularly being looked at to test that they are fit for purpose, and 2020 has seen a Joint Insolvency Committee consultation on changes to SIPs 3, 7 and 9.

These are:

• **Statement of insolvency practice 3.1 – individual voluntary arrangements;**

- **Statement of insolvency practice 3.2 – company voluntary arrangements;**

- **Statement of insolvency practice 7 – presentation of financial information in insolvency proceedings; and**

- **Statement of insolvency practice 9 – payments to insolvency office holders and their associates.**

Further information and background to this consultation can be found at:

https://www.icaew.com/regulation/insolvency/sips-regulations-and-guidance/consultation-on-statements-of-insolvency-practice

The consultation commenced on 27th April and closed on 20th July 2020. The results of that consultation and the possible amendments of the SIPs will be forthcoming over the coming months and careful monitoring of any changes will be required.

7   Brexit

As can be seen from this Chapter, apart from the Act, there is a lot going on in the corporate insolvency and restructuring world. In that regard the 31st December 2020 is also going to be a significant date. Although we may have seen this topic slip down the political agenda because of COVID-19 in recent months, the significance of this country leaving the European Union is huge in terms of the legal and practical consequences for business. In that regard, insolvency law is no different.

As we all know, the United Kingdom left the European Union on 31 January 2020 at 11pm GMT. However, the impact of this departure has, for many business areas, been postponed due to the transition period provided for in the Withdrawal Agreement. This transition period will end on 31 December 2020. The Withdrawal Agreement provides that during transition, the UK continues to be treated as if it is still an EU member state for the purposes of a range of directly applicable EU legislation which is core to the smooth running of financial transactions. So, for insolvency professionals, the recast European Insolvency Regulation ((EU) 1215/2012) ("EIR") will apply to insolvency proceedings opened before the end of the transition period.

The Insolvency Service is very aware of that and has been planning for various scenarios. At this stage, the actual terms of the United Kingdom exit from the European Union have not been finalised, so this book cannot set out any definitive law. However, time is ticking. On 30 June 2020 the Government laid the Insolvency (Amendment) (EU Exit) Regulations 2020 (the "2020 Regulations") (SAI 2020 No. 647) which implement the Withdrawal Agreement and remove the conflicting provisions contained in the previous Insolvency (EU Exit) Regulations 2019 (the "2019 Regulations") (SI 2019 No.146).

This provides some short term relief, but is not the final answer. Since this piece of European legislation is based on reciprocity, there is clearly no guarantee that from 1st January 2021 insolvency proceedings in this country will be respected elsewhere in Europe. There could also be increased uncertainty for English insolvency practitioners seeking the assistance of courts in different European countries.

From the United Kingdom's point of view, agreeing something as close as possible to the EIR would be beneficial to all countries. Without a new treaty or treaties between the Member States and the

United Kingdom, then recognition and assistance in insolvency cases will be governed by either certain common law doctrines, or by invoking s.426 of the IA 1986 which provides a statutory power to assist upon request of a foreign court. However, this does not include all countries. There is also the UNCITRAL Model Law, which is located in the Cross Border Insolvency Regulations 2006 (2006/1030), but again not all countries have ratified this.

If none of these are in play, then insolvency office holders seeking recognition and enforcement of orders in other jurisdictions will need to rely on the local laws.

Clearly, insolvency deserves serious further post Brexit consideration. The current harmonious relationship through the EIR with other European countries is mutually beneficial and important in many insolvency cases where assets are in multi jurisdictions.

As with all areas of law, it is important to keep fully abreast of potential developments.

8   Conclusion

As can be seen from the above brief analysis, there is a huge amount of change and potential change for the insolvency professional to come to terms with.

It is hoped that this book has helped in a small way to guide busy practitioners through the developments. Probably more so than ever, the work of all involved in this area is extremely important, as the insolvency and restructuring profession seeks to help so many affected by this tragic pandemic and assist in the management of the uncertainties of business and professional life in the foreseeable future.

MORE BOOKS BY
LAW BRIEF PUBLISHING

A selection of our other titles available now:-

'Covid-19, Homeworking and the Law – The Essential Guide to Employment and GDPR Issues' by Forbes Solicitors
'Covid-19, Force Majeure and Frustration of Contracts – The Essential Guide' by Keith Markham
'Covid-19 and Criminal Law – The Essential Guide' by Ramya Nagesh
'Covid-19 and Family Law in England and Wales – The Essential Guide' by Safda Mahmood
'Covid-19 and the Implications for Planning Law – The Essential Guide' by Bob Mc Geady & Meyric Lewis
'Covid-19, Residential Property, Equity Release and Enfranchisement – The Essential Guide' by Paul Sams and Louise Uphill
'Covid-19, Brexit and the Law of Commercial Leases – The Essential Guide' by Mark Shelton
'Covid-19 and the Law Relating to Food in the UK and Republic of Ireland – The Essential Guide' by Ian Thomas
'A Practical Guide to the General Data Protection Regulation (GDPR) – 2nd Edition' by Keith Markham
'Ellis on Credit Hire – Sixth Edition' by Aidan Ellis & Tim Kevan
'A Practical Guide to Working with Litigants in Person and McKenzie Friends in Family Cases' by Stuart Barlow
'Protecting Unregistered Brands: A Practical Guide to the Law of Passing Off' by Lorna Brazell
'A Practical Guide to Secondary Liability and Joint Enterprise Post-Jogee' by Joanne Cecil & James Mehigan

'A Practical Guide to Crofting Law' by Brian Inkster
'A Practical Guide to Spousal Maintenance' by Liz Cowell
'A Practical Guide to the Law of Domain Names and Cybersquatting' by Andrew Clemson
'A Practical Guide to the Law of Gender Pay Gap Reporting' by Harini Iyengar
'A Practical Guide to the Rights of Grandparents in Children Proceedings' by Stuart Barlow
'NHS Whistleblowing and the Law' by Joseph England
'Employment Law and the Gig Economy' by Nigel Mackay & Annie Powell
'A Practical Guide to Noise Induced Hearing Loss (NIHL) Claims' by Andrew Mckie, Ian Skeate, Gareth McAloon
'An Introduction to Beauty Negligence Claims – A Practical Guide for the Personal Injury Practitioner' by Greg Almond
'Intercompany Agreements for Transfer Pricing Compliance' by Paul Sutton
'Zen and the Art of Mediation' by Martin Plowman
'A Practical Guide to the SRA Principles, Individual and Law Firm Codes of Conduct 2019 – What Every Law Firm Needs to Know' by Paul Bennett
'A Practical Guide to Adoption for Family Lawyers' by Graham Pegg
'A Practical Guide to Industrial Disease Claims' by Andrew Mckie & Ian Skeate
'A Practical Guide to Redundancy' by Philip Hyland
'A Practical Guide to Vicarious Liability' by Mariel Irvine
'A Practical Guide to Applications for Landlord's Consent and Variation of Leases' by Mark Shelton
'A Practical Guide to Relief from Sanctions Post-Mitchell and Denton' by Peter Causton
'A Practical Guide to Equity Release for Advisors' by Paul Sams
'A Practical Guide to Unlawful Eviction and Harassment' by Stephanie Lovegrove
'A Practical Guide to the Law Relating to Food' by Ian Thomas

'A Practical Guide to Chronic Pain Claims' by Pankaj Madan
'A Practical Guide to Claims Arising from Fatal Accidents' by James Patience
'A Practical Guide to Subtle Brain Injury Claims' by Pankaj Madan

These books and more are available to order online direct from the publisher at www.lawbriefpublishing.com, where you can also read free sample chapters. For any queries, contact us on 0844 587 2383 or mail@lawbriefpublishing.com.

Our books are also usually in stock at www.amazon.co.uk with free next day delivery for Prime members, and at good legal bookshops such as Wildy & Sons.

We are regularly launching new books in our series of practical day-to-day practitioners' guides. Visit our website and join our free newsletter to be kept informed and to receive special offers, free chapters, etc.

You can also follow us on Twitter at www.twitter.com/lawbriefpub.

Printed in Great Britain
by Amazon